What Others Are Saying about This Book . . .

A gem of a book; endearing, engaging and inspiring.

—Catharine Hamm, *Los Angeles Times* Travel Editor

A cleverly told real-life adventure story. Terrific!

—Diane Bruno, CISION Media

More than a titillating travelogue, *Amazing Adventures of a Nobody* is a sojourn into the psyche of America. In his masterfully conceived expedition, Leon is forced to gamble on the grace of humanity, with inspiring results.

—Brad Klontz, co-author of *The Financial Wisdom of Ebenezer Scrooge*

Masterful story telling! Leon begins his journey as a merry prankster and ends a grinning philosopher. Really funny—and insightful, too.

—Karen Salmansohn, Oprah.com relationship columnist, AOL career coach, and *NY Times* bestselling author of *Bounce Back Book: How to Thrive in the Face of Adversity, Setbacks and Loses*

A thoroughly funny and wonderful story! This is a thoughtful book, and a whole lot of fun!

—Aura Imbarus, author, *Out of the Transylvania Night*

Brilliant! An "amazing adventure" and hilariously good fun!

—Steve Hudis, Producer Impact Motion Pictures

A compelling and rich travelogue that ultimately opens our eyes to the human connection.

—Sharrie Williams, author, *The Maybelline Story —and the Spirited Family Dynasty Behind It*

This book is fun, fun, fun!

—Nina Siezmasko, actress, *The West Wing*

There are life lessons in this book that will serve you well in business. A most important read.

—Kolie Crutcher, CEO and publisher, *Get Money Magazine*

Very real, readable, inspiring, simple and at the same time, like all great writing, goes quickly to the core of human nature.

—Ted Klontz, co-author, *Mind over Money*

The humor in this book makes it a fun read, but the social commentary makes it an important book.

—Charmaine Hammond, author, *On Toby's Terms*

A great read, and who knows, you may find your true calling by the end of it all!

—Stephen Viscusi, America's Workplace Guru and bestselling author of *Bulletproof Your Job: 4 Simple Strategies to Ride Out the Rough Times and Come Out On Top at Work*

a life changing journey across America relying on the kindness of strangers

leon logothetis

www.BettieYoungsBooks.com

Disclaimer:
This is a true story, and the characters and events are real. However, in some cases, the names, descriptions, and locations have been changed, and some events have been altered, combined, or condensed for storytelling purposes, but the overall chronology is an accurate depiction of the author's experience.

Front cover design: Dunn+Associates, www.dunn-design.com. and Damon Kidwell
Author photograph by Jesse McLean, Jr.

BETTIE YOUNGS BOOK PUBLISHERS
www.BettieYoungsBooks.com

Bettie Youngs Books are distributed worldwide. If you are unable to order this book from your local bookseller or online, you may order directly from the publisher.

Distributed by SCB Distributors
15608 South New Century Drive
Gardena, CA 90248
800-729-6423
www.SCBdistributors.com

Library of Congress Control Number: 2010915368

ISBN: 978-0-9843081-3-2

10 9 8 7 6 5 4 3 2 1

Printed in the U.S.A.

To Dr. Susan Mann,

Thank you for believing in me.

Contents

Foreword

A few years back I set out on a trek to "find myself." My travels had taken me to many places, and on one particular night, I found myself all alone, in a tent, high in the mountains of Montana. I hadn't seen or talked to another human being in more than two weeks.

Surrounded by the darkness of these lush green mountains, I was plunged into a solitude I had never felt before. Even my trusted friend, my diary, seemed to have turned her back on me. This was long before the days of smart phones, iPads, and Gameboys, and my futile attempts to distract myself were for naught. I didn't know what to do. So I ran. I struck camp in the dead of night, hiked several hours back to the car, and drove for more hours, in a manic attempt to find another human being to interact with. Anyone.

The ironic thing was that my trip had actually been successful. I had indeed found myself. Now that I had found me, I had no idea what to do with him. I knew I was running from myself, but had no further wisdom about what to do with my new found friend.

That's my story. This one is Leon's.

I have known Leon for a number of years. I am not sure I have ever met a man as insatiably curious as he: humble, bright, creative, delightful, engaging, adventurous, loving, caring, passionate, generous, fun loving, graced with a good dose of being willing to face the world's dark energy—as well as his own. These are the adjectives I would use to describe his beautiful spirit.

Like all of us to some degree, Leon has been on the eternal journey to answer life's great questions: Who am I? Why am I here? Where am I going? What am I to believe? What's this life thing really all about? What's the true nature of this human experience that I am subjected to? Is there a meaning beyond *us*? Is the universe, indeed, a friendly place or not? (Albert Einstein has been quoted as saying the answer to this specific question is the most important we will ever ponder.)

Most of us don't stray far from our comfortable lives to answer these questions. We may travel to seek the answers, but not many of us as pilgrims or supplicants might, which is what Leon chose to do. His journey began with no food, no money, and not much of a plan.

Leon has had the good fortune to have traveled the world as he has sought these answers and indulge in what many of us wish we could give ourselves permission to do. He gives us the opportunity to go with him through this book, to give us some ideas about what our options could be, if and when we might run into ourselves.

Find out what Leon did, and then ask yourself, "What would I have done?"

This is a masterfully told story about a man, who, unlike me, didn't run.

—Ted Klontz, co-author of *Mind Over Money*,
and *The Financial Wisdom of Ebenezer Scrooge*

Acknowledgments

Writing this book has most certainly not been a one man show. I have had plenty of help along the way. It is here that I want to pay tribute to those who carried me on this journey toward becoming an author. Without the love and support of my family I would have struggled to dedicate my time to this book. I will always love my mother, father, and my three brothers George, Con, and Nick: "One for all and all for one."

I owe a huge debt of gratitude to Dr. Susan Mann, for it is her encouragement that showed a hopeless young kid that he did indeed have *value* and could become whatever he wanted to be.

Angela, the safest person in my life. I will always love you.

My grandmother whose love and affection I have always cherished. Thank you for loving me.

I owe a great deal to my publisher Bettie Youngs for having enough confidence in and patience with this first time author. Without your support and guidance I wouldn't have the honor of authoring this book. I promise to calm down for the next one! Thanks also to the sensitive copy editing of Elisabeth Rinaldi, and for the design and layout by Jane Hagaman of Quartet Books, and others from Bettie's staff who had a hand in bringing this book to press.

Jason Ashlock my good friend, thank you for your wisdom and friendship. Matt my editor extraordinaire! What can I say, you helped craft this story and I am forever grateful for your creativity and dedication.

TC Conroy, my secret weapon. Your insight, patience and support have helped me to become the man I am today. Thank you.

These acknowledgements would not be complete without mentioning Kute Blackson. Kute, I cannot thank you enough for everything you have shown me. I look forward to our next adventure in Shiri.

I would also like to thank all the people I met along the way who helped me successfully complete my journey across America. Without your kindness and generosity of spirit this adventure would never have been possible.

Last but not least, my best friend in the whole world, Winston! You taught me how to love and for that I will be forever grateful.

Introduction

The Way It Was

Once a day allow yourself the freedom to dream.

—*Albert Einstein*

I admit it. This whole thing started because of an Argentine Marxist revolutionary, a depressing London flat, a subtitled foreign flick, and a personal existential crisis. Sounds like a combustible combination, I know. And it was. It was also the beginning of something beautiful. Here's the thing no one tells you about an existential crisis: when you're in the middle of one, happenings strange and slight can take on meanings they would never have possessed prior to the moment when you're sitting on your couch wondering why you're alive, why you were born, and if anyone would really care if you disappeared. But at that moment—with empty beer cans, crushed potato chips, and a dead cell phone scattered about your flat—the world becomes a collection of symbols: things tiny and normal come to represent ideas large and new.

So it was when, after finishing year number five in what seemed an interminable unfurling of a lifeless, meaningless career, I sat down in front of the television one evening. "I don't have a bad life," I told myself again and again, like one of those horrible daily affirmations. "I should be happy, right? I have a home, a job, more money than I need, a dad and mum and brothers who care about me, even if they don't readily share such feelings. . . ." But somehow none of it felt real; it felt, I suppose, like it wasn't even really my life. I hadn't built it, hadn't fought for it, hadn't erected a real, true life for myself from the elements of passion and longing. I was lonely, yes, but not just for friends or lovers. Honestly, I was lonely for me. Sounds silly, I suppose, but all these years I'd lived with me, and never felt like I was really there. And now, here I was, in front of the television on another dull and foggy London night, considering the fact that if I disappeared, the world would be the same, I'd have left no mark upon the planet, no lasting legacy in someone's life, and that I would not be missed, even by me. To chase the thought from my mind, I picked up the remote and clicked on the television.

And I had what every filmmaker hopes his audience will have when he shoots and edits his work: an epiphany.

I'm not an intellectual. I don't speak French, I don't know how to pronounce *Sartre,* I don't speak the language of –isms, and until the night I saw *The Motorcycle Diaries* I would have identified Che Guevara as the pleasant chap who stood next to his donkey on the tins of cheap coffee. And, I'm not a crier. Or I didn't used to be. I rarely felt touched by films, I never got teary-eyed at weddings or birthdays, and I never, ever, *ever* wept while lying on a therapist's couch. I'm a Brit. We may suck at global domination, but we're good at stoicism. Really good. Check out the Queen: the blasé raised to the level of art. So boring it's captivating.

But that's the thing about an existential crisis. All of the sudden, things change. Big questions get asked. Grown men cry. And lives are altered. For just over two hours, I followed Che Guevara (played by Garcia Bernal) as he traveled across Latin America—from Buenos Aires to Caracas—with nothing but his trusty motorcycle and his close friend Granado. That journey changed Che, and for that matter, history. What happened to those two young men as they wandered the bleak terrain of mid-century Latin America transformed their understanding of the world—and their understanding of themselves. Che would never be the same. The poverty, the weariness, the kindness, the largeness of the world, and its beauty and brokenness, put the fire in his eyes that we still see in his photographs—that distant longing and determination, that knowledge that he was born for something greater than his small past or his sleepy present.

I've never considered myself a revolutionary. And I'm pretty much a pacifist, I suppose (though I'm a little shaky about any label that ends in –ist). But Che got to me. The experiences he had along his journey quickened a part of my soul that had until that time remained dormant. I felt the powerful potential of human connection in all its glory, as these two free-spirited friends wound their way into the hearts and minds of so many eclectic strangers. As the credits rolled, I left my flat, my blood moving quickly as I bounded down the stairs on a wave of adrenalin. *Something* inside me had awakened and, in that moment, the fresh air of the London streets filled my soul with hope. I had no grand social vision, but I sensed the need for revolution, if only within myself.

It dawned on me that my world was defined by accumulation, by the gratification of acquiring things, of seeing numbers go up and go up again. Accustomed to and enamored of such trappings, I had completely neglected the internal voice that had been sweetly crying for my attention. On that windy November night, I started listening. I was alone. Having worked for half a decade in a business run by my family, having accumulated a respectable sum of money and respect from my peers, having found myself an impressive flat in an impressive neighborhood, I realized I had no motorcycle, and I had no Granado. No trusted companion and no vehicle to carry me into the larger world. Though I'd felt the absence of both long before Che roamed the countryside on my television, I had never allowed myself to confront what the lack of deep human connection and adventurous exploration meant: my world and my heart were too small. As I walked the cold London streets, I felt lighter with each step. I began to formulate a plan. Mission: see the bigger world, find deeper connections, build a bigger heart, grab a Granado, and find the real Leon. How? On a metaphorical motorcycle.

"And you think," My father asked, looking, fittingly, incredulous, "Your plan will work?"

"I guess it depends on what you mean by *work*," I replied.

"Is that a riddle? Are you doing the Buddhist riddle thing already? Shouldn't that wait until you're in Tibet, or wherever you're going?"

I only smiled a reply, which I thought a very Buddhist thing to do.

My father is a pragmatist, and that has its own kind of

virtue. He comes from a long line of pragmatists, all of whom looked a son or a brother or a nephew in the eye at some point in their lives and asked, "And you think this will work?" I doubt my answer was as good as any of theirs.

I'd worked as a broker in my father's firm for five years. He'd been good to me, offering me the spot, and he'd been rough on me, too. The hours were long, the work myopic. It was in this office, in this building, despite its large glass windows overlooking the city, that I'd lost my perspective on the world. It was here that I'd lost myself. And it was time to change.

"I'm leaving in two weeks," I told him. "So, I guess this is my notice."

"Fine. I accept it. I cannot, of course, promise that your job will be here when you get back."

I smiled again.

"And I, of course, can't promise I'll be back."

Two weeks after quitting my job, I realized something. The accoutrements of a modern urban life are not easy to divest. Said another way: when you own a lot of rubbish, it's tough to simplify your life. If my desire to revolutionize my inner life was to be more than a dream, I needed to make some drastic reductions. Reducing, however, is quite counterintuitive these days. The word "less" isn't our favorite. To do something counterintuitive, sometimes you have to enact arbitrary rules, strange and perhaps irrational guidelines to force yourself out of a way of life so habitual it feels like instinct.

Before I traveled across a continent, before I signed a potential television deal, and before I stumbled into a new life, I determined to strip myself—metaphorically, that is; I haven't the physique for the real thing, or the stamina. I committed to remove myself from my normal environment and experience a world as far removed from the stifling routine of business meetings and expense reports as possible. To keep from falling into my old habits of isolation, I would travel in such a way that I would be forced to connect with others. I started big and worked my way to the small, identifying the forces that had kept me from experiencing real human connection and seeing the world:

My country. A Brit in England is like a cowboy in Texas. If he wants to be anything other than what his father was, he needs to cross the border—or several borders. So I left behind the biggest little island in the world. Headed to the place where reinvention isn't just a possibility, it's an expectation: the United States.

My car. I am a fan of keeping the earth green, but that's not why I sold it. I worked and lived between walls, separated from the world outside and the people who populate it. If I was going to travel, I was going to do it without a big piece of metal between me and the air and the life.

My clothes. They make the man, and they make the man forget he's more. I wore only the ones on my back, and kept a fresh set in my trusty backpack.

My money. Technically, I did not give this away. I only forfeited my access to it. No cards, no cash. Each morning, I'd ask my producer to give me five dollars. He'd hand it over, with no chance of getting more and no chance of the money carrying over to the next day—I couldn't accept money from anyone; only acts of generosity could help me along my journey. In the pages that follow, I don't focus on the money, because it wasn't the point: Five dollars is nothing nowadays—it disappears like water. I might as well have had nothing, and many days, it felt like I did.

My lifelines. No cell phone. No e-mail. Only my lungs to shout for help, and my legs to carry me from danger or to rescue. There were, of course, those camera guys hanging around, but God be my witness, they were about as unhelpful as those stiff-necked, flat-chinned chaps at Buckingham Palace. And the crew wasn't *allowed* to help me. While I hoped for a roof over my head, and was often on the verge of sleeping on park benches or sidewalks, they'd stay in fancy hotels. While I tried to cobble together a meal of whatever leftovers people might offer me, they ate at the finest restaurants.

I brought them with me to document my journey, but they ended up serving a much larger purpose: they were the image of my indulgent, comfortable, former self. They were my foils.

I felt in my bones that something extraordinary would happen and I wanted to capture it so I could share it with the world—so I could pass on the incredible stories I knew were waiting for me. Traveling with a camera crew could have been awkward. It could have ruined everything, I suppose. But not with these guys. They traveled at a distance, and weren't with me for a good portion of the events that happened in this book. You'll see in these pages that they are pretty invisible, popping up only now and again. In fact, it can be honestly said that they played as big a role in the trip as they do in this book: they were watching, silently, while I plunged ahead.

Without the car and clothes and money and phone, I was at the mercy of the one thing no human can go without for long: relationships. It would be relationships that fed me, clothed me, carried me, and cared for me. Without the basic necessities of life, I'd be forced to find a friend; hundreds of them. And I'd be doing so in America, the great land that feels like it's still being discovered. As a metaphor for my own transformation, I would start my journey in Times Square, a symbol of capitalist decadence, and end my adventure at the Hollywood sign, where people flock to manifest their dreams.

A radical experiment? Yeah. But in my opinion, there's no better way to respond to an existential crisis than by doing something radical. There's no better response to the realization that you're a nobody than to do something amazing. There's no better reply to monotony and the mundane than adventure.

When this chapter began writing itself (chapters do that, I swear), it assumed it would be an opening. "Introductory matter," my agent said. ("Huh?" I said back.) But I'm breaking the rules. I will tell you how this book will end.

When you reach the final page you'll see I've shed the toxic environment of my old life. You'll see me in California, a continent and a half (yes, England's the half, pint-sized speck of land that it is) from where I began. You'll see I've gone from working behind a slab of wood for sixteen hours a day, pursuing a life someone else had chosen for me, through a pilgrimage of self-discovery. You'll see me trade in my luxury car and overbearingly pretentious briefcase for a pair of walking shoes and a back pack. You'll see me exchange self-sufficiency for the grace and companionship of total strangers.

You'll see me share a hotel room with a woman who was convinced she was the target of a hired assassin and that the F.B.I. was building a drug factory under her house. You'll see me stand in disbelief after having been given the keys to a complete stranger's house with an offer to "make myself at home" while she was away. You'll see me spend a sleepless night in a curiously blood soaked hotel room, and pass up a chance to camp in the desert with a skeleton of a man who spoke only in whispers. You'll see me rap with local gangsters in a tree-lined suburb of Illinois. You'll see me traveling with Iraqi war veterans through the stream-choked mountains of Colorado. You'll see *me.*

That's where the book ends. You seeing me. Me seeing you. The kind of exchange we lose if our eyes aren't open to each other. I left London clinging to my old life of privilege and routine. I returned infused with a thirst for connecting to my fellow human beings, a commitment to living an authentic life, and openness to experiencing fully the unpredictable and joyous adventure of the open road and the open heart.

This is my motorcycle diary, my journey through the heart of the United States, in search of its soul, and mine. I found both.

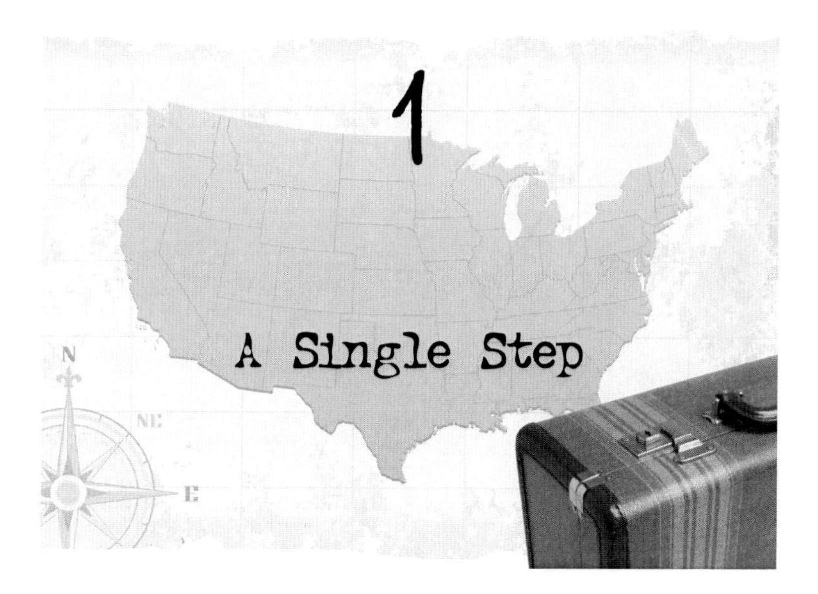

Bite off more than you can chew. Then chew it.

—Ella Williams

I do not want to hide behind the magical thinking that isolating will solve all my problems. This destructive belief keeps me tethered to my past. I have to make a conscious decision to live from a place of integrity and personal strength. This is my time.

-From my journal, en route to America

It seems to me that, generally, humans travel for two reasons: we are pushed, or we are pulled. A broken levee floods our neighborhood, pushing us out, forcing us elsewhere. Or we are offered a job we can't refuse, and are pulled to a new city, drawn to opportunity. We break up with a lover, and are pushed out of a town, feeling we can no longer stay in a place that holds too many memories. Or we fall in love, and are pulled to follow that fall to a new place, where another life can begin. We are pushed; we are pulled. Something always gets us moving—even if we don't know exactly where we're going.

I could tell you what pushed me—a desperate sense of isolation that seemed incurable in London, and a job that seemed only to encourage it. But I had trouble explaining what was pulling me. It was all abstract, I suppose, and terribly idealistic: I wanted to feel connected to people, to experience the meaning of the human family, to find a reason to believe in the kindness of strangers. I wanted to leave the solitary confinement of my London life and leap into the great huddling mass of the American multitudes and be greeted by the optimism and unity and shameless happiness of the Western world's wonderland of hope. America had always inspired me. I'd grown up with shows like *The A-Team*, beckoning me to an America that was magic, the land of the possible. And now, I was heading head-first into its vastness. In today's global village, through times of cynicism and economic tribulation, this truth has somehow remained: there is no place on earth that remains a more powerful symbol of hope than does the United States.

I didn't expect the first person to embrace me to be a pimp from New Jersey.

Times Square. The perfect starting point in my quest to travel across the U.S. The bustle, the crowds, the constant flurry of activity and excitement. What better place to launch my journey? I would meet some folks, make some friends, tell people of my plan to find connection, build relationships, and discover the goodness of humans and the goodness of myself. It would be fun! It would be easy! I would soon be invited to travel with a crowd of pleasant college students, or a lovely family headed back to Jersey after a show, or embraced by a delightful group of young ladies who had ventured into the city for a soiree of music and dancing! My imagination ran past my reality. "Look!" I thought, "Plenty of people, all ready to offer human connection and comfort." I would be headed toward Hollywood in no time.

It took five minutes for me to realize this was a monumental miscalculation.

The people moved past me in a blur, bumping into me on either side. "Excuse me . . ." I'd start, only to have them rush onward with the masses. "I'm sorry, but do you have a moment . . ." I'd begin again, only to be hustled out of the way by a group of foreign tourists. "I wonder if you could help me . . ." I said a little louder to a group of middle-aged women in "I Heart NY" T-shirts, only to be met with an offhand, "Don't look him in the eye, Brenda."

Let me say this about people in Times Square: most of them are smiling. This is because they are either selling something ("Hey, you like stand-up comedy? Check out the show tonight . . .") or buying something ("Look, Dad, *wicked* T-shirts! Can I have one?"). It is a separate world from the rest of America, an island within an island, a volcano of light and consumerism. My producer Nick suggested that before I begin, I should make a pronouncement for the record, a speech to inaugurate my journey, and perhaps people would stop and listen. I might gather a crowd, he said. I might rouse them into a cheer. So I stood proud as

I could and tall as my frame would let me, and announced my intentions to the throngs.

But in such a bustling environment, a foreigner announcing his intended journey across the country isn't exciting. It's forgettable. I might as well have been holding a cardboard sign and a plastic cup. Soon I was just another voice in the crowd, a sideshow that wasn't nearly as interesting as the naked cowboy or the flying green woman. I thought perhaps I should start dancing or singing, if only to get people's attention. So I did. This was the only time the people in Times Square stopped smiling.

And it dawned on me, there on the corner of 44th and Broadway—the NYPD station behind me, and the absurdly oversized flashing signs competing with the early morning sunlight—that my great idea of traveling America relying on the kindness of strangers was going to be one hell of a hard time. Ten minutes into my experiment, and the panic was already rising in my throat. Hundreds of people were swarming about, each of them lost in their own thoughts and conversation, their eyes lifted to the advertisements above them. A large man gesturing wildly to get the attention of his family bumped into me hard, knocking me into a woman passing the other way with her hands full of bags. I was a pinball in an angry machine, and the beads of sweat began to form on my bald head.

What I had gotten myself into?

I needed to think, and God knows, Times Square is not the place for thinking. So I did what I have always done when I needed to think: I started walking.

I walked south, then west, to anywhere, to nowhere. The crowd thinned and the lights dimmed. "Be reasonable," I thought. "Make a plan. You can do this." It seemed reasonable to me at the time, though I would soon learn better, to seek out standard travel arrangements. In these initial hours, I was still playing by the old rules, with self-reliance as my default. I had a lot of miles to cross between New York and California, so I started where one should start: the bus terminal.

"Where to?" asked the man at the ticket window.

"Good question." I hadn't thought my journey would start this way: *alone* at a bus station. I was flummoxed. I swallowed. "How about . . ." I scanned the Port Authority schedule board. "Charlottesville, Virginia!" I said, my voice falsely cheery. Four hundred and sixty miles from New York, the schedule indicated—an early sign of my irrational mood. Attempting to travel 460 miles in one day with only $5 in my pocket was about as likely as persuading Mick Jagger to spend the rest of his life in a Catholic monastery.

"That'll be $68," said the man through the tiny hole in the glass.

"I have . . . five."

"Five what?"

"Five dollars."

"That'll get you a cab to Columbus Circle. . . . If you're lucky."

"And if I told you that I am a distant relative of the Queen and in need of some authentic American generosity?"

"I'd tell you to call Her Highness and have her send a plane."

"Right-o, my good man . . ." I decided to play up my Britishness. Don't Americans like Brits? I considered. Our accents, our charm, our nifty manners? "Might there be any chance of a free bus ticket? I shall invite you to tea when next in the city."

"Man, stop messing with my time. If you ain't got no money, you ain't getting on the bus. And I don't want no tea."

"Cheerio, my good man."

"Yeah, yeah. Tea and crumpets and all that."

Dejected, I left the Port Authority, and stumbled back into the streets of Manhattan. I had only one option, and I struggled to even form the thought in my mind: I have to ask for help. For someone who had spent the majority of his life avoiding connecting with others, I was about to experience something new.

I honestly could not remember the last time I had approached anyone for assistance—for *anything*. You see, the British don't ask for help. We just get on with our lives, retain the stiff upper lip, and live with whatever comes our way. It took Chamberlain quite a while to hold up his hand and ask for a bit of help with the little problem of the Third Reich. It's generally agreed upon to be a ridiculous strategy, to go it alone. It gets us into trouble emotionally because it violates the first rule of human connection: opening yourself up to others inspires a chain reaction. It's simple in theory but excruciatingly difficult in practice. I had lived my life shying away from showing myself to others. Now I was forced to reveal myself at my most vulnerable. It all seemed so much more interesting in the abstract.

"Excuse me, sir, do you have a min—"

If the asking was rather uncomfortable, the rejection was also excruciating. The bus station crowd looked at me as though I were in the final stages of leprosy or high on crack—or both. Being ignored was tough, but being spoken to was worse. When someone did deign to address me it was in one of three forms: civil disregard ("Not interested" or a mumbled "Sorry"); the verbal brick wall ("Don't talk to me!"); or impressive anger ("Get out of my face. Now!"). I actually cringed at a few of these, apologized at a few more, and nearly wept at one or two. After an hour spent looking for someone who was willing to simply talk to me, I began to consider the possibility that I had made a big mistake. If I was going to receive the same reception throughout the rest of the country, I was screwed.

I sat down in the middle of the dirty floor ("dirty," in fact, does not even begin to describe it; I am still working on a word to capture the intensity of its filth), considered the first few hours of my journey, and had for the first time a feeling I would experience frequently during the first few days of my journey: I felt utterly alone.

This was familiar. Aloneness had been a constant companion in my life. Why had I thought America would be any different? Each pair of feet that passed me by reminded me of the life I'd lived so far, and how far I had to go, and how little I had to rely on. Why was I doing this? What was the purpose? Did I really think it was going to be easy? The harsh reality of being refused any kind of support by my fellow human beings was a huge slap in the face.

But wasn't this what I wanted? To learn something? To be provoked to consider who I was and why? Journeys towards the center of one's being are not vacations.

And slowly it became clear: the disregard I met with at the Port Authority was a gift. It provided a vivid reminder of how estranged from others I felt in my everyday life. The only difference between the feelings of being rejected by hostile New Yorkers and my disconnected world was that with each averted gaze and dismissal, I was staring my frailties in the face. I could no longer deny the power of disconnection. At home I could find ways to forget that power:

playing video games, surfing the Internet, aimlessly walking around shopping centers. But here I had to rely entirely on connecting with people to survive.

It dawned on me: my little ploy might actually be working. True, I might not have actually connected with anyone—yet—but now I *wanted* to. I had to. And that seemed as good a place to start as any.

A moment later I saw them. Well, first I heard them.

"Hey baldy!" the guy shouted at me.

Looking back, I suppose I should have been frightened. But I'd just had an epiphany, and the endorphins were rocking. I spun around and saw my angels of mercy—a black couple who looked like they were ready for a street fight, or had just finished one—which turned out not to be to far from the truth, as I would soon learn. In any other situation, I might have paused, stumbled backward, and ran from the terminal. But this was the first New York life form that had shown the slightest bit of interest in me, and I felt I couldn't waste the chance. Who cares if he looked a little hostile? He had ice cold eyes, but seemed almost . . . jovial, and a bit happy to see me. He was wearing a New York Yankees hat and oozed confidence like I did sweat.

"What are you doin', baldy?"

"I—I don't suppose," I stammered, "that you could, um, buy me a ticket to Newark . . ." (I had lowered my expectations and decided to try and get the eleven miles to Newark instead of the 460 to Charlottesville.)

"Dude," the stocky man interrupted, "Why?"

"Why?"

"Why should I help you? Why should anyone help you? What are you giving back? This is *New York,* man."

"Well, I tried singing and dancing—"

"Ha! Nah, man. I mean, you gotta have a story."

I thought for a moment, and offered my hand. "I'm Leon. And I will do whatever you want; I will say whatever you want to hear. If you buy me a ticket to Newark, you will become like a brother to me."

He and the woman both laughed. "Yeah, yeah, but I *got* a brother. What I wanna know is, where's the story, man?" he asked.

"It's all about how you package yourself," his female companion said.

"Package myself?"

"Yeah, man. You want this, you gotta work for it."

It was starting to make sense. My newfound tutors were knowledgeable folk. I thought back to any one of the homeless people I'd seen on the street in London. Any of the dozens that I'd passed on any given day, holding their signs, or singing their songs, or playing their instruments. I thought about the boldness that prompts people to approach you in the Tube, telling their story and asking for help. It was the story and the performance that convinced.

And so I spilled it: I explained in overwhelming and unnecessary detail the reality of my situation, why I had left the comfort of my home in London to traipse around America. They got more than they'd bargained for.

"Well, that's a start!" the man laughed. "Look, Dom, baldy can tell a story!"

I smiled. "I'm Leon."

"I'm Don."

"Dominica," said his partner.

We all shook hands. Don squeezed hard.

"What other advice can you give?" I asked as we started walking.

"You have to . . . *sell* yourself," she said firmly. "You have to make people notice you before they're going to help you. You might as well be hiding behind the trash can, the way you're quietly sliding around."

"So I'm basically invisible?"

"Pretty much."

Ah, a revelation.

I *was* invisible, and in fact had long cultivated and cherished that invisibility. Being a ghost had its privileges—no social responsibilities, no chance at vulnerability, no worrying about the rest of the world. I had lived for far too long in the shadows. Here I was in New York meeting my first potential angels and they could already see what I couldn't: I was a ghost in the world and my life was being lived in the shadows. It was time to become human, even if it was scary.

And it was. No sooner had Don and Dom Fox become the first people to help me along the way, the bliss was abruptly interrupted by angry shouts from a pair of extremely large men. Their puffy coats and oversized jeans exaggerated their bulk, and the pace at which they were moving made it seem they were on us before I had time to size them up. They walked in unison, synchronized in their stride and their facial expressions communicating one simple message: we are big, and we are angry.

"Ummmm . . . .D-D-Don?" I whispered.

"Shit," Dom said. "They've been following us all the way from Brooklyn."

"Who . . . who are they?" I asked.

"Pimps," she whispered. "They think we're trying to take their turf."

"Oh. Pimps. Lovely." My journey did not include plans

for becoming a New York statistic. A Los Angeles statistic would be far preferable. If I were destined to be murdered, I'd prefer it happen by the ocean, in victory, after having achieved personal enlightenment. Far more poetic than the streets of Manhattan.

In seconds the menacing pair reached us. "What the fuck are you doing on my turf?" the taller one exploded, going toe-to-toe with Don. I've rarely seen two men's noses touch, and it was a frightening sight.

Dominica stepped between them with an easy grace and explained that she and Don had simply been passing through Brooklyn on their way to Manhattan. Don backed her up, standing directly beside her, a unified front. I stood off to the side, feeling like some kind of unclaimed prize. The voices rose higher, louder, and I looked around for a place to hide when the inevitable shootout began . . . rubbish bin, garbage can, sewer. I decided on a conveniently placed lamppost and wished myself thinner.

It was over in thirty seconds. After a few heated words, the pimps turned and swaggered off. A turf war had been averted, apparently. I emerged cautiously from my slender hiding place.

"What did you say to them?" I asked.

"I told them that if they didn't leave us alone," Don answered bluntly, "I would stab them."

"Oh. Stab. Lovely." My head was spinning.

"No one fucks with me, Leon."

"Uh-huh." My legs nearly buckled.

"I'm just kidding with ya! No man. I just told them they had the wrong people and to leave us be. No biggie."

I chuckled nervously, as Dom and Don erupted in howling laughter.

"Come on, man, let's get you to Newark!"

"Newark? But I only have five dollars."

"It's Newark, man, not Chicago. It only costs $1.50 on the PATH."

So after being abused by countless New Yorkers, barely avoiding a panic attack, and finding myself embroiled in a gangland altercation, it turns out I could have paid for a ticket myself. At that moment, it seemed the funniest thing in the world, and even Newark seemed like the Promised Land.

Still basking in the first real connection I had managed to create, I looked at Dom leaning on Don's shoulder. On so many levels we did not have much in common. They were street smart New Yorkers and I was an Englishman who lived as far away from the street as possible. There was some magic here: it cut through our perceived differences and hit a tender spot deep within, a spot not visible to the naked eye. The magic of human connection is that it transcends all classes and upbringings. The separations we create for ourselves are only that: a creation. At base we are all one and the ability to connect with another human being dissolves the illusion of separateness. This is indeed magic.

And this invisible man was beginning to see it.

2 Brotherly Love

No one can whistle a symphony.

—H. E. Luccock

"And what about you, Leon? What'll it be?"

The wrestling mat held a couple dozen of my classmates, eleven-year-old boys dressed identically in short white trunks and blue-collared shirts, and all of them staring at me, impatient for my answer. Mr. Goldstein was staring too, his big eyes unblinking, his wrestling whistle swinging from his neck, bouncing off his large belly.

"Well?" he asked again, this time a little louder. "Leon? When you grow up to be a man, what will you be?"

I didn't have an answer. Everyone else seemed to have a plan, or at least a dream. The usual—doctor, lawyer, banker. The unusual—marine biologist, safari guide, architect. But

I felt nothing akin to the certainty or optimism my fellow chaps in gym class demonstrated. What did I want to do with my future? I did not know I even had a future.

But I opened my mouth to speak anyway. Hopeful, I suppose, that my tongue would know better than my brain, and something interesting would emerge from my chapped lips. Nothing did.

"That's okay," Goldstein said a bit more quietly, as I exhaled in relief. He looked around at the class. "We all know that Logothetis is a bit thick, and won't make much of himself. Likely he'll live off his father for the rest of his life."

There was a restrained chuckle from the boy to my left, outright laughter from the others, and squirming from them all. I sat still, my eyes on the floor. It was the first time I remember feeling completely alone.

If Times Square is Happy Land, Newark is the Republic of Melancholy.

"So this is New Jersey," I said, descending the train-station stairs and looking out into the asphalt abyss. Dom and Don stopped on the bottom step, both of them with their hands in their pockets.

"Yep. In all its glory." Don said. "What do you think?"

"I wouldn't exactly honeymoon here." A sad, skinny dog trotted across the street and into an alley.

"No!" Don laughed, and clapped me on the back. "Me neither! Let's get moving."

As pleased as I was to make the first steps of progress on my journey, the deserted streets of Newark seemed unlikely to celebrate with me. It was a very small victory anyway: it had taken me almost a full day to travel eleven miles, and I hadn't eaten or drank anything since I'd begun my odyssey. I was hungry, slightly parched, and already growing nervous about the next step.

A familiar feeling was creeping up on me: I was ready to be alone. I was ready to thank D&D, give a quick handshake and half-hug, and go on my merry way, back to the world of self-sufficiency. I'd gotten lucky with Dom and Don, having found a compassionate couple who showed me a bit of unique kindness. What was the likelihood that angels like these would find me again? I'd proved my point: random kindness existed, and I had been its recipient. Did I really have to go on? And how?

I was opening my mouth to suggest a preemptive farewell to D&D when a priest turned the corner and nearly knocked me over.

"Well, hello!" he said cheerfully. "Sorry about that!"

"No worries," I answered. "No harm done."

"Have a pleasant evening," he said, as he continued down the street.

"You, too. . . . Wait—."

This couldn't be coincidence. Just at the moment I'm about to turn back, to give up, thinking I can't once again approach complete strangers and ask for handouts—despite D&D's attempts to train me—I run head-first into a man of the cloth. "I wonder . . ."

He stopped and turned to me. "Yes?"

"I—I wonder if you could . . . help me get a bus ticket for Charlottesville."

He stared at me, his eyes large and unblinking.

Logothetis is a bit thick, and won't make much of himself . . .

The pause was long enough that D&D began to shift beside me in awkwardness. I was about to turn and walk away, if only to get away from that penetrating stare, when he reached out his hand.

"And what's in Charlottesville?" he asked.

"I don't know exactly," I said, shaking his hand. "It just seems a reasonable next stop."

"On your way to where?"

"To L.A."

"Tell him, baldy!" Don said from behind me.

The priest smiled. "Tell me what?"

I turned to D&D and then back to the priest. "Well, you want to hear a story?"

"Always," he said, leaning up against the brickwork of an abandoned building and crossing his arms with a grin.

I spent a few minutes explaining my situation—London boy crawls out of cocoon and travels the U.S.A. to discover the kindness of strangers and the possibility of human connection—trying to keep to the important details, and not to go overboard with too much of a sob story. I could feel Don peering over my shoulder, ready to call me out if I descended too deeply into self-pity.

The priest seemed genuinely interested, smiling and nodding appreciatively. I had hit the right button with a priest, I thought, with my tale of social integration and cultural reunification. I reached the climax and returned to my earlier request for a ticket to Charlottesville, with confidence that free passage was soon to be delivered.

I was wrong.

"Great story, Leon. But I can't help you there," he said flatly.

"Oh." My disappointment must have been evident. "Well, okay then."

"But I like you, Leon. And I think you've found yourself an interesting hobby."

"Thanks. It beats wrestling, I guess."

"What did you say?"

"I used to wrestle in school. Hated it. Sort of represents to me the worst possible option."

The priest laughed much louder than I expected, and I couldn't help but smile, despite not understanding what was so funny.

"Sorry," he said. "It's just—that's my hobby."

"I'm sorry?"

"Wrestling. Of sorts. I'm a submission fighter."

I turned to D&D, who were clearly as shocked as I was: I had stumbled onto the only professional wrestling priest in the whole of the Western world.

"Then how about this," I began, my mouth running ahead of my brain. "If I can pin you down, will you buy me a ticket?"

"Are you kidding?" he asked, perplexed.

"I think I can take you!"

"Oooh!" I heard Don getting excited.

The priest paused and looked at me hard. "Okay," he said, and I saw a fiery flash cross his kind face.

I moved quickly, going for his legs. He danced backward a half step and slipped his hands around my arms, twisting one behind me. In a flash I was in the air, my feet above my head, and then suddenly on the ground, my face in the dirt and my chest pressed firmly against the grass. My ears ringing from the force of the tackle, I could hear D&D's fits of laughter echoing somewhere above me. It was clear that the fight was over before it had really begun.

"Can we get a count?" the priest asked to no one in particular.

"One!" hollered Don through his laughter. "Two. . . . Three!"

The priest released his grip and rolled me over. Still stunned, I stared up at him standing over me, his hand outstretched, the kindness back in his eyes.

"Nice try," he said with a grin.

"Thanks," I moaned, taking his offered hand and stumbling to my feet. I dusted the dirt from my jeans. "So no ticket, eh?"

"'Fraid not," he said. "But how about something better?"

He placed his hand on my shoulder, bowed his head, and began to pray.

"God, let your blessing, your covering, come over this gentleman, my friend Leon. May he be safe in his travels. May he have faith in you. And when he is weak, may you keep him strong. Amen."

He looked up, and we locked eyes for a moment. "You're gonna be all right, Leon. This is America. You can make anything happen. You can make anything you want of yourself."

He gave me a firm hug, slapped me on the shoulder, and trotted off, perhaps to wrestle religion into some other unsuspecting stranger. I turned back to the bleakness of Newark—my spirit calmer than I'd felt it in a long while—to see what D&D made of the situation.

But my traveling companions were nowhere to be found.

By the time I'd circled the neighborhood and wandered into the train station, more than an hour had passed, and

I was coming to terms with the fact that Don and Dom were gone for good. They disappeared as quickly as they'd come, and I felt the strangest sensation: I missed them. There'd been, for a few hours, a kind of partnership among us—something we loners don't find very often—and as I scanned the faces in the station, I realized I was unlikely to find another pair like them. I'd never see them again, and even now I wish I had some way to find them and offer my gratitude. They were the first of so many unexpected blessings. I was ready to find the next.

My brief sparring session with "Father Bruce Lee," as I'd call him from then on, left me a little bruised and my right shoulder sore, but the mystical power of prayer and biological phenomenon of adrenalin still lingered, and I was feeling hopeful. There was a spring in my step as I walked toward a woman seated in the waiting area. I'd just wrestled a priest; what marvelous adventure was awaiting me next?

"That's a nice hat," I said cheerily.

"Oh," she looked up from her paper. "Why, thank you."

"Is there any chance . . ."

One thing I learned quickly on my journey: some people are just born generous. It's in their blood, their D.N.A. They are natural givers, like birds fly and fish swim. Life offers them chances to do what they love to do, and they do it. My lady friend in the hat bought me a ticket to Philadelphia. It wasn't because I was charming or handsome. It was because such gifts were what she lived to give.

We are not separated from others, we only pretend to be. This illusion leads to all manner of rudeness. When we wake up from our trance of isolation and see our connection to the world, we realize that when we offer help to others, we are really helping ourselves. The generous among us already know this.

My ticket in hand, I walked to the track, put one foot in the car, and looked back over my shoulder.

"Farewell, Newark," I said, waving to no one in particular. It wasn't a beautiful city, and no place for a honeymoon, that's for sure. But sometimes treasures are hidden in the most unassuming of packages.

When people ask me for advice on traveling the U.S., I tell them to take the train. Or the bus. Americans love their cars, those little private boxes, tiny islands of metal and glass and petrol that transport them from place to place providing limited interaction with strangers. Automobiles are efficient, sure, but they offer little in the way of serendipity. Ride in a car and you know what to expect: backseat battles between the kids, fuzzy radio stations, feet on the dashboard, fast-food wrappers on the floor. But ride in a bus or on a train, and you're met with surprises at every turn. You never know who you'll meet or sit by or what you'll overhear. There's magic in allowing yourself to be surprised.

The woman across from me on the train from Newark to Trenton was loudly instructing the elderly and apparently hard-of-hearing man seated next to her in the correct way to roll a joint. The man two rows back was writing lyrics for a new track on his self-produced hip-hop CD. And the train attendant who passed through the aisles taking tickets was celebrating the birth of his first son, showing off pictures to passengers he'd never met and would never meet again.

In Trenton, I switched to a bus and sat down next to a sharply-dressed young black man, and held out my hand. "Hi there, I am traveling to Los Angeles to touch the Hollywood sign. What's your story?"

After a quizzical look, the young man took my hand. "I'm Duval," he said, "from Haiti."

"A long way from home."

"Both of us, it appears. I live in New York now, though. Headed to visit my sister outside Philly."

"So we're a bit alike, no? Both non-Americans . . . outsiders."

"I suppose so. What's in L.A.?"

"Do you want to hear a story?" It would become a kind of refrain for me. He smiled a yes, and I told him my tale, though it had just begun.

"And what have you learned so far?" he asked.

"How to avoid being shot and that living the American dream is difficult when you are penniless," I replied with a smirk.

Duval chuckled. "I reached more or less the same conclusion my first week in America!" Then he reached in his pocket and pulled out some cash, ready to make the kind of gesture on which I had gambled the success of my entire adventure: an act of kindness to a total stranger. He handed me a ten dollar bill.

"When you get to Philly, go and buy yourself ten cheeseburgers on me." I reached out instinctively, but hesitated when my hand touched the paper.

"Sorry, Duval. Believe it or not, I can't take your money," I said with teeth clenched. I could nearly taste the imaginary cheeseburgers.

"Oh, well . . . do you accept credit card donations?"

I laughed. "I don't think so."

"Money order?" he suggested with a grin.

"Nope . . ."

Then, Duval had a brainstorm: "What if you purchased my ten dollars with your five dollars."

"Duval! You're a genius, my friend!" This kid was gonna make it in America. "But I'm afraid I can't. Just tangible gifts," I said. "Food, transportation, lodging, maybe clothes—that's it."

"Those are tough rules. Whose are they?"

"Mine. I made them up. Kind of wishing I hadn't . . ."

Duval stuffed the bill into his pocket, and a few minutes later we said our farewells as he hopped off a stop or two outside Philadelphia. I looked out the window as the city approached. Cars, exits, and telephone poles flew past, symbols of connections and communication that I had lost. The seat next to me was empty now, and I found myself feeling lonely. I wondered if I would have the opportunity to make deeper or more lasting connections with the people I met, or if my journey would be a collection of passing conversations.

The bus dropped us near what must have been Philadelphia's Chinatown, where the language barrier between me and the passing crowds served as a perfect metaphor for the distance I had felt between myself and others most of my life. I was a stranger in a strange land, and nothing was mine—no face recognizable, no voice familiar. It was as if the universe had given me a physical manifestation of my isolation: here, in Philadelphia's Chinatown, I was as alone as I would ever be.

I unfolded a map outside a small traditional Chinese market and counted the blocks to a nearby youth hostel. What better place to connect with people than a youth hostel, crammed to overflowing with poor, itinerant adolescents, each on a grand existential journey? It would be the exact opposite of this lonely Chinatown walk.

Unfortunately, some ideas are better in theory.

I sauntered up to the rather dreary hostel, sweaty and hungry, and faked as large a smile as I could.

"Hey, mate," I said to the desk clerk. "I'm Leon, and was wondering if you could spare a free room for the night."

"Excuse me?"

I explained my plight, highlighting the spiritual side of the journey, the reliance on kindness from the strangers I met along the way, hoping if I could connect with him on a deeper level he might be more inclined to help me out. "So what I'm saying," I concluded, "is that you can be part of something momentous and beautiful, man." I felt like a hippy.

Unfortunately, there was no free love here. "Why should I help you?" he replied. "In fact why should anyone help you? Let me tell you something, man. You have absolutely no chance of getting anything for free, okay? This is Philly."

"Right! The City of Brotherly Love?"

"Ha!" He turned to some guests gathered on the ratty couches. "D'you hear this guy? City of Love." They chuckled, and I felt my face turn red. "Listen, man, you thick-headed or something?"

We all know that Logothetis is a bit thick . . .

"Hey, this is twenty-first century America. You got money, I got rooms. You got speeches, I got a door that opens right behind you, and I suggest you use it."

My eyes were on the floor and I heard an "Oooh" from a kid sipping something from a bottle encased in a paper sack. I looked over and saw him elbow his buddy and point my way. This was familiar: the feeling of disconnect, of being alone in the room. I'd been here before, I thought.

We all know that Logothetis is a bit thick . . .

I shook my head, my past connecting with my present. I'd learned my lesson early—if you don't open yourself to others, they can't hurt you. And here I was, on a journey that would demand I continue to make myself vulnerable in order to establish some kind of connection with others. I smiled. This time it would be different. The oddest feeling welled up inside me: instead of discouraging my efforts, the clerk's tirade and the laughter of the kids on the couch were actually making me even more determined to succeed. I waved at them all, and walked out the door, glancing back over my shoulder to see the clerk return to his paper. Was I an idiot to believe that there was kindness in the world? Not only that it existed—I already knew it did—but that there was enough of it to support me, to carry me across a continent?

Philadelphia's beautiful in the evening. The setting sun skips off the river and casts the buildings—the ancient edifices and the glimmering glass skyscrapers—in a terrific orange and yellow. I walked through downtown, finding myself near the art museum and Rocky's statue raising his hands in perpetual triumph. When I hit the Hollywood sign, I thought, I'm raising my hands just like that.

Rocky. The ultimate self-made man, drinking his eggs, and punching the cold meat. Those two stubborn souls, his coach and his wife, who refused to give up on him. He was a lonely soul that rose to triumph through a remarkable feat of will and the loving support of companions. It was possible, this thing I was trying to do.

But it wouldn't be easy. The clerk had asked a pretty important question: Why *should* people help me? If people did help me along the way, what were they getting out of this? I knew what I wanted, but what did *they* want? Or did they want anything in return? It seemed to me, as I watched twilight descend upon the city, that people—at their core—strive to be generous and good, but our society makes them fearful and thus more introverted. We become unable or unwilling to show our true selves. My journey was a contrived experience, yes; but it was meant to lay the foundation for a different kind of interaction. I wasn't going to lower my protective shield unless I forced myself into an experiment, like Che and the motorcycle. My journey was my classroom: I was learning about myself and those around me. And I was betting that at least some people would get the chance to learn about themselves, too, through interacting with me; we'd be each other's pupils and teachers.

My ruminating had taken me about twelve blocks, but gotten me no closer to a room for the night. I needed to get practical: further reflection was not going to get me a place to sleep. It was at this point that my night took a rather unexpected, but welcome, turn.

I passed a small house with an open window, where a young guy—maybe twenty-two or twenty-three—sat by the window playing on his computer. Against my better judgment, I decided to approach, to strike up a conversation with a complete stranger minding his own business in his own house.

"Hallo!" I said cheerfully. The young man's head whipped away from his screen to the window. I held up my hands, palms facing the surprised fellow. "I'm very sorry to bother you, and I know I look like a psycho, but I'm not. Basically, what I'm doing is going round the U.S. on five dollars a day to prove I can rely on the kindness of strangers. I've had a very long day and am pretty much totally desperate, and though I don't even know your name, I wonder if you could help." He reached toward the drawer of his desk. "Jesus! Do you have a gun?"

"No!" he said, pulling out a pack of cigarettes. "I haven't got a gun. Even though it is America."

"Well, that's good news." I took a few steps closer. "In that case, can I possibly—how do I say this?—can I stay on your couch tonight?"

"I work at, uh, seven tomorrow." He flicked the lighter and lit the cigarette, exhaling toward the window.

"Does that—so, can I—what? Can I stay?" I said excitedly.

"Till then," he said.

"Sorry?" I was in shock.

"Till then," he said, louder and crisper.

"Till seven tomorrow?" I could hardly contain myself.

"Yeah, sure."

"Are you being serious?" I just wanted to make sure this guy was not smoking crack.

"Yeah."

"Man, I need to hug you!"

"That'd be kind of awkward through the window."

"I'm Leon." I reached my hand through the opening, and he shook it.

"Derek," he said. "Well, Leon, you're rather convincing. See you at the front door."

While Derek moved through the house, I proceeded to run manically down the street punching the air with both fists and yelling sweet words of joy to anyone who would listen. I was absolutely ecstatic and felt a great sense accomplishment; not quite believing yet that my audacity had paid off. Here I was, a shy Englishman unable to talk to people in my everyday life yet perfectly willing to speak to a complete stranger to ask him to stay in his house. I felt a surge of pride and adrenaline course through my veins. I had taken a risk and was on my way to staying the night with a complete stranger. When I arrived at the door—back from my dance of joy—I couldn't help but praise the American spirit.

"My God, so this is American generosity, huh?"

"I guess so. You want some pizza?"

I laughed. "Yeah, man. I want some pizza! I'll buy you a drink!"

We walked a couple blocks to a local pizzeria and I handed Derek my $5. Pepperoni had never tasted so good.

Derek worked in a government job and seemed to be immersed in the techie world, as his house was rigged with electronic gadgets of all different shapes and sizes. He gave me a brief tour, attempting to explain some of the hardware he was obviously very proud of.

"And this is the setup, man. Right here. This is the World of Warcraft station."

"What's that?"

He looked at me in shock. "What's World of Warcraft? You don't know?"

"I don't think so . . ."

"So you don't play?" He was showing more surprise than he had when I approached him at his window. "I thought everybody played. Well, it's this entirely other world . . ."

He spent about fifteen minutes explaining "this entirely other world," and I did my best to listen. The least I could for my host, I thought. He was passionate about the game, but not simply the competition of it. He was drawn to the connection, the sense of team and community.

"And when I'm on, I'm connected to millions and millions of people around the world . . ."

My eyes lit up. I understood. Not the game—Lord knows I had no clue how to play. But I understood the sense of excitement he felt when he logged on. One moment he was alone. With a click of the mouse, he was among friends.

"That sounds pretty amazing," I said, when it seemed he'd concluded.

"It is, man. It really is."

My energy was fading, and sleep was calling. Derek could tell.

"So what happens tomorrow?" he asked.

"This will all start again."

"Man, I don't know how you do it."

I didn't know either.

Derek gave me the couch, said goodnight, and went to bed. As I lay there, reflecting on the day, I felt extremely grateful. A young computer geek had saved my night and shattered many of the misconceptions I had about the youth of America. I fell asleep amid the blinking red and green lights of computers and gadgetry.

The next morning I woke up and gobbled down a half frozen bagel. It wasn't good, but who knew where my next meal was coming from? Two days into the journey and I'd already learned not to pass up a free bit of food. Derek's job awaited, and we said a hasty farewell on his porch before I wandered forth into the city. I tried to thank him as profusely as I could, but he just waved it off.

"I only ask one thing in return," he said.

"Anything!"

"When this whole thing is over, check out World of Warcraft. You don't know what you're missing." I nodded in agreement, and we shook on it.

I smiled and waved as he walked off, and turned my head toward the great metropolis.

I had to find my way to the crew's hotel to retrieve my daily allowance and let them know I was heading off. It wasn't as easy I thought. The city around me was brimming with life, full of skyscrapers and busy streets. I stopped and asked directions in a couple of shops but the clerks seemed less interested in me when they realized I wasn't buying anything. I'd spent the last of my money with Derek the previous night, and the experience of being unable to walk into a shop and buy a drink or a pack of gum, or anything for that matter, was definitely a shock to my system. Along with most of the Western world, I had gotten used to dipping into my pockets to find a few notes or coins to buy everyday things: coffee, mints, newspapers. I had never felt so removed from my everyday routine. I felt helpless.

By the time I found my crew's hotel, I was sweating and a bit panicked. Derek and his World of Warcraft and bagel already seemed a long time ago. I stepped into the lobby of the magnificent Loews Hotel, and dozed off in a chair while I waited for the crew to wake-up from their beauty sleep. I would soon realize that being on the periphery of luxury—like sleeping in the hotel's lobby instead of in one of the lavish rooms—would become a staple of my travels. I was destined to be the proverbial outsider, always looking in.

The crew finally came downstairs and took great pleasure in describing their encounters with jam doughnuts, creamy milk, huge pineapples and fresh, hot coffee. Under normal circumstances this would probably have upset me. But I was fully aware that this was one of the main reasons I had invited them along: I wanted to be reminded of the "other side of the street" as a way to increase the impact of having nothing but my wits, resourcefulness, and ability to bond with people to help me along this journey. If it meant that I had to meet the crew every morning and be regaled about their scrumptious eating habits and their five-star accommodations, so be it. My journey was about transcending the external luxuries that I had been accustomed to most of my life. It was an inward journey surrounded by external temptations every step of the way, and the crew were physical representations of the man I wanted to leave behind. Their jam doughnuts and fresh coffee only served to increase my focus.

But then again, this was only day two.

I left the hotel and wandered off to the central bus station, passing several people who appeared to be in various degrees of poverty. An elderly woman with unkempt hair, a baggy dress, and rolled-down stockings muttered to herself as she stumbled past. A man (at least I think it was a man) dressed in stained pants and a torn shirt darted between pedestrians with his hand out, begging for change.

Without taking time to think it through, I hurried to the station manager's office to ask for the person in charge. Two rather old ladies were waiting in the office, their bags neatly placed beside their chairs. I smiled at them, and they looked me up and down like I was their rebellious grandson before turning their gaze to the hulking man who had just joined us.

"Can I help you, sir?" his name tag said Max and his title was "manager." This was my man.

"You certainly can!" I gave him my spiel. He listened, somewhat interested, to the bald English man. I told him that I was looking for a handout: a free ticket to Richmond to be exact.

He turned to his comrade, a skinny bearded fellow with a bowtie and a clipboard. The two of them exchanged a glance, maybe a telepathic conversation, and then turned back to me in unison.

"Yes," he said with a hint of a smile. "We'll give you the ticket."

"You're kidding!"

He just laughed, and I hugged him, and he laughed harder. I turned to hug the two older ladies, but the look on their faces did not seem to welcome an embrace.

This was too good to be true: today I would cross the famous Mason-Dixon Line to begin my experience of southern culture—and hopefully, more of my much needed American hospitality. Minutes later I was holding a free ticket to Richmond, with a stopover in Washington, D.C., where I was told I would need to change buses. I was about to visit the nation's capital, symbol of democracy throughout the world, and I'd gotten there by doing nothing but asking for a helping hand.

Waiting for the bus outside the station, I looked around at my fellow passengers-to-be. Some asked where I was headed and why, and upon receiving my answer, expressed admiration—and a dash of doubt.

"You're very brave!" said a young mother with a screaming baby.

"You're a better man than I," a heavyset, middle-aged man said, shaking his head and puffing on a cigar.

"Not better, mate," I suggested. "Just crazier."

"I'll drink to that," he eagerly agreed.

I chuckled.

"Nah, I'm serious. Got any booze?"

"I bloody wish!" I said. "But my budget doesn't allow for luxuries."

"Mine neither!"

I joined the clustering group at the bus door. Evidently we soon would be boarding, and I wanted to sit at the front so that I could strike up a conversation with the driver—I never knew when the next random act of kindness was going to enter my life, and my only strategy was to stick close to the people who I thought could help me along.

Unfortunately the bus driver was uninterested in my advances. His lack of response to my chitchat quickly led me to believe that it was best for both of us if I just shut up. I sat back and was asleep in no time, and before I knew it, we were on the outskirts of D.C. I looked out the window, hoping to see a familiar landmark—the Washington Monument perhaps, or the grand dome of the Capitol. Nothing. This was the back side of D.C., I supposed. And it wasn't grand at all.

When we switched at the D.C. bus terminal, I spent a few minutes in the gift shop. I spun the postcard rack and stared at the glossy images of the city's landmarks. Lincoln in his chair; that great white needle reaching toward the sky; the four men planting that flag at Iwo Jima. I pulled out a slick picture of a uniformed guard standing over a tiny eternal flame. I held it up and stared at the yellow fire. And then I looked out at the crowd in the station. Families with children; men with rucksacks; teenagers with backpacks bigger than themselves. I leaned against the door of the shop and wished for a camera. This was the American I wanted to know: the average man, the average woman, the average kid. The people who do nothing spectacular other than wake up in the morning and make a life, make a family, make a community. I didn't need to view monuments or to read speeches from great men or halls of power. I needed this: to be surrounded by people, to look at them not as threats or inconveniences or distractions, but as individuals whose journeys were not unlike mine. We were all of us wandering America, relying on each other more than we sometimes knew.

I grabbed my bag, threw it over my shoulder, and slid the postcard back in its slot. I didn't need a souvenir. In front of me were people I could know and I aimed to meet as many as I could. Here, in the backside of D.C., where no one visited, was the real eternal flame. Somebody, I thought, should take a picture.

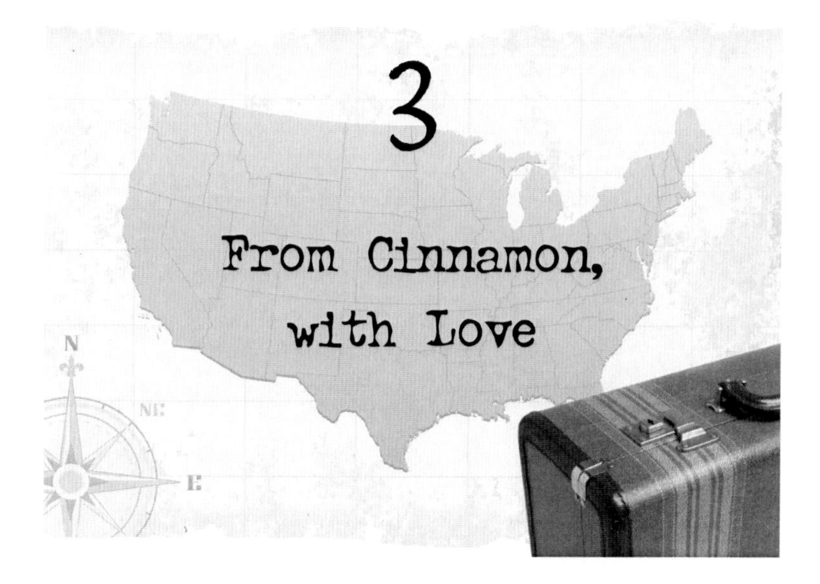

3
From Cinnamon, with Love

The odds of going to the store for
a loaf of bread and coming out with only
a loaf of bread are three billion to one.

—Erma Bombeck

Traveling is good for us for many reasons, but I'm convinced one of the reasons we like it so much is because it places us in a position of control we don't often find for ourselves in our daily lives. When we're home in our routine, we go where we're told, or where we must, on someone else's time, at someone else's pace—to work, to school, to the shops, to the meeting. But when we travel, we go where we wish. We eat where we want, we stop when we're ready, and we start up again when we feel like it. Traveling is marvelous because we have some semblance of control over life's pace—and with it comes a sense of accomplishment at every turn. You cover miles, you move along, you check off sights seen and places passed, you travel linearly toward a particular destination, on your own particular timetable. In all of us, it inspires a sense of achievement and ownership.

But what happens when a trip has no predictable end? When there is no itinerary? What happens when the control we enjoy in travel is stolen from us—or willingly sacrificed? Letting go of this measurable travel, and the sense of control that goes along with it, deepened my sense of dependence on others. My trip across America accomplished a radical shift, both away from my life, of course, but also away from a typical sense of travel.

My father is a traveler. During my youth, he was gone as much as he was around, always jetting off to Brazil and Greece and beyond. His work was in shipping, and the job called him away frequently. I recall being six or seven and watching him pack, demanding that I go with him to wherever far-off place he was headed. Rebuffed at every turn, I climbed into his luggage, wishing myself small enough to stow away among his suits and shoes.

I never got to go with him to any of his far flung destinations. I watched him go, and I watched him return, his suitcases heavier upon return than upon departure. He'd bring back exotic items—an old hunting rifle from South Africa, a sleek tortoise shell from Vietnam. And he brought back stories as well, of loud and colorful cities, of people who spoke a language we could not even mimic, of land and water more beautiful than London could offer.

Though we never joined him on his trips, my family did take one annual journey together. If my father had wanderlust, there was still one place that had a hold on him as home, a place that always called him back. It was the place of some of my earliest memories of the beauty of a foreign landscape—and also of my growing tendency toward isolation.

On the island of Chios you are as close as you can get to Turkey while still claiming you're Greek. And it's a place that will make you believe in the beauty of rocks. Seriously—if you ever thought large boulders were dull, go to Chios. Soon you'll be hugging them more than a hippy hugs trees. Rocks take on personalities on Chios; they have names and sometimes faces, and they beg you to come touch them, to climb them, and if they're small enough, to pick them up and take them with you. With their smooth whiteness and welcome cool relief from the hot Mediterranean sun, you'll soon think of them as friends.

I spent every summer of my childhood on Chios, in a small town by the sea called Komi. My grandmother's house still stands there (when I visit her, I sleep in the same bunk bed I did as a child). So rich are my memories of that place and the sunny days I spent hopping atop the rocks and swimming in the sea that I have informed my living kin that should I die, I wish to be cremated and my ashes scattered across the village rocks.

Though I best remember it as a joyous place, those rocks hold one harsh memory. One sunny afternoon my brothers and I were playing with the village boys—inventing some game of territory and team—bounding off the boulders and running red-faced across the rocky soil. At some point the game changed—I was never sure who made up the rules—and I was left on the wrong side of the group's spontaneous law. Suddenly the game I knew was taken from me; I was out of control, and the group was against me, my older brother among them. I can't remember who first picked up a small rock and tossed it my way, but I remember the feeling of the pellet against my skin, and the prick of several more thrown harder each time. There, against the backdrop of the stunning blue water, my friends and siblings were throwing the rocks of Greece at me. Like some sad biblical child who disobeyed a tribal law, I was being stoned.

I ran to my mother, shouting hysterically while the boys laughed and scattered. My arms and legs were red, my head was bleeding. She wrapped me in her arms, and pressed a cool rag on my head and calmed my breathing. My father walked in and saw me, pathetic and betrayed.

"What is this? What happened?" he asked. His eyebrows were narrowed and his jaw set.

I tried to explain as best I could, between the heaving and stuttering, but I couldn't understand myself, much less describe, the group's mad turn. What had I done? I wondered. Where had it gone wrong?

"You boys," he said as he turned away. "I cannot take you anywhere . . ."

I didn't know it at the time, but it was a defining moment: the birth of mistrust. The group that one moment embraces you can turn on you the next. I pulled away from my mother and ran off to be alone. I wanted to run forever, to continue on until I was someplace else, where the ones I had so foolishly trusted could not touch me, could not hurt me. Looking back, it was the first time I connected traveling to escaping. As I wandered alone for the few hours before dusk, the thought formed in my mind for the first time: perhaps my father did not travel because work forced him to. Perhaps he traveled to run away from the only ones who could hurt him. Traveling was a way to be safe and alone.

Shaking the memories of Chios and Komi from my mind, I turned to the day ahead, noting the irony of my current state of travel: once I had thought of travel as a way to be alone, and now I was traveling with the sole purpose of connecting with people. I chuckled to myself, but stopped when the woman seated in front of me looked at me strangely. I just nodded at her, straight-faced. She wasn't in on the joke. Neither was I apparently. At least not entirely. Someone else was delivering the punch lines.

As the bus weaved its way through the suburbs of Richmond, for the first time since I began my journey, I was approached before I could even start searching for a kind soul to hit up with my story. An attractive brunette in her mid-thirties came and sat next to me and smiled. "Hello stranger! Where are you headed on this fine day?" she blurted out. She had a terribly contagious grin.

"Uh . . ." I was taken aback by having been beaten to the punch. "Richmond?" I replied sheepishly, stating the obvious, since we *were* on the bus to that very place.

She laughed her reply. "Well, congratulations! You've nearly made it!"

I was confused. Not about where I was going—that had settled in—but about the conversation. I was still shaking off the bout of melancholy my memories had plunged me into, and couldn't figure out who this woman was and what she might want. But I quickly regained my composure and stuck out my hand.

"I'm Leon. Who are you and what's your story?"

"I'm Karen," she said as she shook my hand hard. "And I'm on the run, Leon."

I was taken aback by this and not completely sure whether to laugh or cry. She touched my arm and leaned toward my ear whispering earnestly, "Please call me Cinnamon."

I laughed.

But she didn't. She looked at me with penetrating eyes. "Someone is trying to kill me. So I changed my identity."

I didn't laugh any more. This lady was being serious.

"Um . . . who wants to kill you? And why would anyone want to? What on earth have you done?"

She refused to tell me who her would-be-murderer was, but this didn't stop her from elaborating on her brush with the nameless assassin. I was concerned for this woman's sanity—but she seemed extremely poised and even lucid. I decided to suspend my disbelief. Isn't that what I was doing on this trip to begin with? Tossing aside my skepticism in my own ability to connect. With this in mind, I allowed myself to be taken on some kind of ride by my new friend Cinnamon. I wasn't sure where we were going to end up, but it's not every day you get the chance to spend a few hours with a lady on the run.

Cinnamon explained that her would-be-murderer was subject to jealous outbursts of frightening intensity and moments of shear madness that would take you to the depths of hell. She had begun fearing for her life after discovering that she was being poisoned with chlorine gas piped in through air vents of her apartment.

"Chlorine gas?" I stammered.

"Can you believe it?"

"No." I couldn't.

"He comes to the house every day at four in the morning and puts chlorine inside the air vents."

This was not normal.

"And how—how on earth does he do this? I mean, is he a physicist who knows the intricacies of chlorine poisoning and chlorine delivery systems . . ."

"That's the interesting thing about this, Leon," Cinnamon whispered. "I have absolutely no idea. Look, I know he has connections around the country, especially in Texas. I think they keep him supplied with both ideas *and* toxic substances. I have to get away; it's my only chance of surviving this. If I stay," she turned away, looking over her shoulder briefly, "I will die."

"But Karen—"

"Cinnamon," she interrupted. "Cinnamon. It's crucial."

I held my tongue. After all, what did I know? I didn't even understand my own world. Who is to say that Cinnamon wasn't in grave danger? That she thought she was, was all that mattered now. And the way I saw it, we were a couple lonely travelers, heading across the universe. I was on a pilgrimage of self-discovery, she of self-preservation. Was she crazy? Wasn't I?

So I determined that my role in this situation was to sit and listen and be as generous with my time as she was being with hers. If the stories were in fact untrue then at least I had given her the time and space to air her feelings and grievances with the world. It was a small gift, but it was all I could offer her. Connection, after all, comes in all shapes and sizes. I wanted to see it from every angle.

"Does he know that you know?" I asked.

She smiled sheepishly. "I escaped as soon as I found out. I have no idea what he knows."

"Why are you going to Richmond?" I asked.

"I'm going to the toxicology center to prove that I am in fact being poisoned and I'm not delusional," she explained.

"None of the social workers, detectives, or government officials I've talked to believe me. So I'm going to prove them all wrong. Everyone thinks I'm lying." I continued my compassionate silence. "Except you, Leon."

It was my turn to smile sheepishly.

"Would you like a cookie?" she asked.

"Would I like a cookie?" I looked at her in disbelief. I was famished. "Well, yes, as long as they're not poisoned with chlorine gas."

We laughed. She had a great laugh. It was real, shameless. "No, I bought these at the store. I don't cook in my house. Not since the F.B.I. started building a drugs factory under my house."

I nearly choked on my cookie, which prevented me from asking the question that was on my tongue: "Are you *crazy?*"

Maybe she was. But here Cinnamon was, wandering the country alone, in an attempt to prove herself. In some bizarre and unexpected way we were both on the same path, a path of proving something to someone. In a strange way, I envied her: she had a clear view of what she wanted. But the question remained for me: what was I trying to prove? And who was I trying to prove it to? My family, my friends, my enemies? I was not sure. But I did know that, like Cinnamon, I wanted to find out who I was and escape the drudgery and failures of my past. If this simple woman can get up and search for a new way of life, then anybody can. The whole point of this trip was to prove to myself that change is inherently a human phenomenon. We can all change. The question is: do we have the will to believe?

The bus finally found its way to the shabby bus depot in the heart of Richmond. I looked at Cinnamon out of the corner of my eye as we disembarked together. I liked her. I couldn't help it. And I admit to feeling a twinge of responsibility for her, too, as though, for however long our paths remained intertwined, it was my duty to make sure she was okay. Parents feel this, I'm sure; spouses and paramours, teachers and guardians. But for me, it was an entirely new sensation. I had never particularly cared to be responsible for anyone but myself. And why should I? People let you down. They abandon you, they run away, they disappear, they pick up stones when you least expect it. I ran from such responsibility in my London life. I had relied on no one there, and no one had relied on me. But here, on this American expedition, I was relying on everyone. It seemed only right that when I started doing that, the reciprocal would occur: others would come to rely on me.

Cinnamon was such an example of the messiness of life, and how within this messiness arrives a beauty that sometimes appears when two souls touch. However briefly this happens, when it does, its magic transcends our dreary reality. Two become one. However far apart they seem.

"So where are you staying in Richmond?" she asked in a small voice.

I realized I hadn't thought about this troubling fact for a good twenty minutes. "Oh," I said, returning to my own reality. "Actually, I have no idea." But I needed to find out.

"Well," she started. "Do you want to stay with me?"

She had uttered seven magical words.

"Uh . . . great! But," I had to be honest, "I probably haven't got enough money to buy a hamburger, let alone a hotel room."

"Oh, don't worry about that. I have enough for both of us."

The streets of Richmond were deserted, and I was beginning to feel that my journey across America would be filled with dark nights and empty streets. I expected to spot Father Bruce Lee under a streetlamp somewhere; the memory of him was enough to make me smile and feel a bit stronger. Dingy motels were everywhere, and when we stepped out on the corner of Frightening St. and Where-The-Hell-Am-I Avenue, I had a deep sense of regret that I hadn't chosen a different generous soul to stick close to. Cinnamon seemed confident, but I was beginning to doubt the sense of loyalty I'd felt to her only minutes before. Roach motels have a way of calling into question your affection for the person you're with.

She led the way at a good pace, and I struggled to keep up.

"Where are we? I mean, which motel are you thinking?" I asked, a bit out of breath.

"I don't know, but we have to keep walking. That guy is following us."

"What guy—" And then I saw him. She was right. A young guy I had seen get off the bus earlier was not more than ten feet behind us.

"Shit!" I said quietly. Oh my god, I thought. Maybe she's not crazy after all . . .

"Hey there," he said from behind us. He must have seen me turn my head.

I turned to him out of instinct. "Hello, mate."

"I think we were on the same bus."

Cinnamon wasn't slowing down, and by this time I was walking backwards.

"Yeah, yeah, that's right."

"Where you two headed?"

"We, uh—"

"Don't—" Cinnamon whispered fiercely.

"Well . . . we don't know yet," I stammered. "You?"

"Just following you," he said darkly. And then stuck his hand in the pocket of his coat.

Shit, I thought. Shit. He's got a gun, a pistol. Or maybe a sprayer, like a mace thing, but with chlorine gas.

"Uh . . . Cinnamon . . ." I muttered.

Finally she stopped and turned, just in time to see him pull his hand from his coat. He was gripping a $20 bill.

"Count me in," he said, pushing the money toward me.

"Excuse me . . ."

"You're the guy traveling the U.S., right? Relying on strangers? Count me in: I will donate twenty dollars to the cause." The money-that-wasn't-a-gun hung between us.

I laughed awkwardly. "Well, thanks, man, but I can't take it, I'm afraid."

He looked at me as though I were an alien.

"Why not? I'm giving it to you. What's wrong with you?"

"More than I have time to explain, I assure you. But right now I just—I can't accept cash. Only food and lodging."

"Oh, I see. So you don't turn into a beggar. Okay. Well, what about this . . ." This guy was a determined chap. "What if I throw the $20 up in the air and turn my back. Then it'll be like I dropped it, you know? And then you can accidentally *find* it, and no one will ever know."

Cinnamon was eyeing him thoughtfully, and I'm pretty sure I saw the beginning of a smile on her face. For a moment I was tempted by the gentleman's offer.

"I'm sorry, friend, but I can't take it. I really wish I could, but if I do, I will have broken my own rules."

"So you're a man of integrity. I respect that. Good luck, then," he said, giving my shoulder a rather powerful slap. "I think you're gonna need it!"

We parted ways at the corner, with Cinnamon a bit less jumpy than before. It seemed kindness can sometimes cut through even the most deep-seated paranoia. Or at least make a few dents.

Cinnamon used another name when she signed into the motel: now, she was Barbara.

"Do you always do that?" I asked, as she put away her wallet and we headed to the dingy elevator.

"Of course, Leon," she said expertly. "Do you know what would happen if they found me?"

I did not know, nor did I want to. It was getting late, and all I wanted was a bed, a pillow, and a few hours sleep to dream of the rolling hills of good old England. Cinnamon, however, had other ideas.

She slid the key card through the lock, flipped on the light, and started on her mission: a thorough military-style inspection of the bathroom. I was waiting for her to pull out the white gloves. She looked under the bed, in the nightstand. She ran her fingers over the sink counter and bathtub, checking to see if the surfaces were clean. She raised the toilet seat, lifted the back of the commode. She checked the closet for a good five minutes, pulled off the chair seats, took out the television remote batteries, and unscrewed the light bulbs in the lamp. When she stood on the desk to check the fire alarm, I had to ask, "Cinnamon, what are you doing?"

She answered without looking at me. "Seeing if they've been here."

Most motels, she explained, were bugged by the C.I.A. She made it a priority to check for these types of devices. She explained how sleeping was impossible until she knew that she was safe and that no one was listening in on her.

"Oh, well, it's a good thing you know what you're doing."

"Oh, Leon," she looked at me from atop the desk. "I always know what I'm doing."

We headed downstairs to the all-night diner attached to the hotel lobby, and I continued to ask myself the same question: Was Karen/Cinnamon/Barbara, in fact, *mad?* Or was she simply a little unbalanced? Or, bigger still, was she not crazy at all, but privy to a truth about America and the world that I simply did not know? I still couldn't tell whether I actually believed the stories she was telling me. At times I felt like I believed, and then she would say something so ludicrous that I would have to quickly return to my senses. My mother used to say you could see if someone was mad by studying the eyes; they would shine a crazy intensity, one that transcended the rational. So far I hadn't noticed that about Cinnamon. But maybe, I told myself, it only came out at night. It was definitely getting dark now.

After burgers and fries and sodas—the most all-American meal I'd had since starting the trip—we found ourselves at the end of our evening.

"Oh, Leon, I have had such a great time!" She flung herself across her bed and leaned up on one elbow. I sat on my bed, more than a little afraid of what might happen next. Surely she didn't think we would . . . or did she? My heart was racing and my mind was on high alert. How would I handle it if she made a move? Certainly she wouldn't have assumed we had some kind of deal . . .

"You are wonderful," she whispered, staring at me intently, her smile softening.

This was not good. Free motel room or not, I couldn't.

"You, uh, you had better get some sleep," I said in my most fatherly voice. "We have had a long day, and tomorrow will be busy, too."

"Ah, yes, tomorrow." I'd distracted her. "Tomorrow . . . You'll come with me, won't you, Leon? I don't want to go to the toxicology center alone."

My heart rate was slowing. We'd avoided the unthinkable.

"Yeah, yeah, of course I'll come with you. But right now, we should go to sleep so you'll be rested and ready."

She turned over and was asleep before the light was out.

I lay with the small lamp casting odd shadows on the far wall. The room was as unfamiliar as any I'd been in—the yellowed paint, the squeaky bed, the lingering sense of must and smoke. I thought about my father, whose life had been spent in hotel rooms around the world, each unfamiliar, each different enough than the next to feel strange, and similar enough to be forgettable. I started a list in my mind of all the places he'd been. What had he seen? The Far East, the Far North, the Sun, and Sea, and Mountains. Then I made a list of my own. The boat trips and plane trips and car trips. He was far away, and yet he was here—with me. He was, I realized in that room, the reason I was here. It was perhaps his best gift, one he did not know he had given, one that prompted me to imagine other worlds and dream of lands beyond my own. It was work that took him places, but travel was never simply an obligation. On the contrary, it seems clear to me now that he chose his line of work based on his desire to see the world. He was always on the move, seeking a new adventure. Though I never went with him, I followed him. Years later I followed him. He'd made me a traveler—first seeking isolation, now seeking connection.

Why hadn't I seen this before? It was obvious now. So disappointed he had been when I told him his career, his company, was not where my future lay. I could see it in his face, hear it in his voice: why would you walk away?

"I can't promise there'll be a job for you when you get back," he'd said the day I left for America.

"And I can't promise I'll be back," I had replied.

We had neither one seen it then. I was only going where he had led me. If the open road called, it was because he had taught me to listen to its voice.

The next morning I stuffed myself at the breakfast buffet with orange juice, milk, cereals, raisins, eggs, bacon, doughnuts, croissant, and waffles. It was a sight—a disgusting one, I'm sure—but I didn't know when I'd eat again. The motel staff were eyeing me suspiciously.

Cinnamon had a solitary cup of coffee, and she drank little of it. I had known Cinnamon for less than twenty-four hours, but I had this strange feeling that we had actually been on this journey for months together. While traveling under extreme circumstances, time can be fused into one long stretch; hours become days, days become months.

The toxicology center was looming large in her mind; her moment of truth was fast approaching. She paid the motel bill and we hopped in the motel shuttle to reach a nearby rental car place.

"Can I borrow your credit card?" she asked.

I was stunned silent. "Uh, I don't have one, Cinnamon, remember? I don't have money at all—"

"Oh, right, right. Well, I'll try this one again, but I don't know how many more times it'll work."

It did, and we were off. My companion's second thoughts about the toxicology center were more serious than I had imagined. She insisted that she did not want to go to the center in Richmond—"They've already gotten to the doctors there," she claimed—and would instead drive us both to Charlottesville, an hour and a half west of Richmond. She was adamant that she would go to the toxicology center there. I highly doubted this, but going further west was going to aid me in my journey so I agreed, counseling her that I would still come to the center with her, no matter where it was.

But we weren't going to make it anywhere with her behind the wheel. After she ran her third red light and veered into oncoming traffic to pass an eighteen-wheeler, I insisted she let me drive. Besides ensuring that we arrive in one piece, my driving had the added bonus that I could get her to tell more of her life story. Thankfully, she agreed. To both.

We took a leisurely drive, spent in constant conversation—well, one-sided conversation. Her life was a veritable smorgasbord of fantasy. She was psychic. She had a relative who was a white witch. The United States had armies on other planets. She could communicate with anyone through history. When she focused, she could make things happen by sheer will. It just kept coming. By the time we arrived in Charlottesville, her voice was raspy from the constant talking, and my head was hurting from trying to absorb the litany of fables.

After driving into town, I pulled over to the curb a few blocks from the historic main square. As I suspected, she'd had a change of heart and did not actually want me to be present at her toxicology test results. I did not press the matter. Perhaps, of course, the whole toxicology thing was a ruse. But bringing that into the open was not going to serve either of us, so I agreed to go on my way.

"Well, Leon, I guess this is good-bye," she said. Her face seemed sad.

"For now," I reminded her. We had talked in the car of meeting up again someday. I really wanted to know how her toxicology tests came out and how life would treat her. She gave me her cell number and I promised to call her when my trip was over.

"People always say that," she said tentatively.

"I know, but they have not experienced the bright light of connection that we have, right? We'll meet again one of these days, I am sure of it. You have to let me know what the results are, after all."

"Okay, I'll try," she smiled, brightening. We shared a hug, and then I hopped out of the car towards an uncertain future.

"Until we meet again," I said through the window.

Cinnamon nodded, blew me a kiss, and drove off, leaving me standing with mixed feelings on the corner.

It's clear to me now, as it was clear to me then, watching her rental car sputter along the road and weave awkwardly toward the center of the city, that for all her issues and anxiety, for all her fables and storytelling, Cinnamon and I had one thing in common: so deep was our uncertainty and isolation, that we would concoct the most absurd scenarios just to connect with others. Sometimes we are so alone and so afraid, so lonely in our own spaces, that we will use any excuse we can find to crash into each other in search of that spark of connection.

4

The Streak

Tell a man there are three hundred billion stars
in the universe and he'll believe you.
Tell him a bench has wet paint on it and
he'll have to touch it to be sure.

—Murphy's Law

At the base of the Blue Ridge Mountains, in the middle of Virginia, sits the sleepy southern town of Charlottesville. With a population of barely over 40,000, it matches village charm with American industriousness, balancing rich history (three American presidents have called lovely Charlottesville home: Jefferson, Madison, and Monroe) with youthful vigor. Now it's best known for two sites that embody the mix: the unforgettably dignified Monticello and the energetic intelligence of the University of Virginia.

I didn't know any of this when I arrived. I didn't have a guidebook, and honestly I didn't care. Cinnamon had just dropped me near the square and I was still pondering all of her unforgettable stories as I wandered through the historic town center. It soon became clear that the sleepy Charlottesville I expected was anything but: it was a vibrant college town. The place was literally packed with students, their sweatshirts boasting institutional pride, and their backpacks crammed with books and who knows what else. They were everywhere, all of them going someplace, none of them in a hurry.

College life never really suited me, as I had always felt myself completely devoid of the concentration needed to succeed academically. Most of my time at university was spent doodling and daydreaming about traveling the world. I graduated eventually, on time if I recall, but somehow always knew those few student terms wouldn't be my glory years. Or at least that is what I had hoped! My experience with books, professors, parties, and sports was defined by the same kind of isolation and withdrawal that had reached its crescendo and driven me to this experiment. Watching these students laugh with one another, study earnestly in coffee shops with their textbooks spread before them, their coffee within easy reach, and cluster at street corners beneath leafy campus trees, made me wonder what I'd missed. Perhaps, I thought, now was my time to find out.

I turned a corner onto a gorgeous tree-lined street full of large white-washed mansions, each boasting a set of Greek letters signifying their affiliation to some large American fraternity. Frat Row, the locals called it, and it struck me as the perfect place to find some kindness. After all, who hasn't seen *Animal House?* The music! The fun! The free beer!

It was around lunchtime, and I was certain that there would be a barbecue someplace. I watched for smoke lifting from behind the mansions, and listened for music coming from each house. I saw no signs of life. Perhaps it was too early. The parties last night surely lasted into the wee hours. The weary young scholars were likely still sleeping.

I waited a few minutes under a large oak, but my breakfast of early that morning was disappearing, and it was time to start hunting for food. And as I'd learned already, it was never too early to start searching for lodging, as that seemed never to come easy. The house nearest me hosted a fraternity that began with a Lambda, which I took to mean good luck—for Logothetis, of course. After all, I was of Greek descent, and surely these, the brightest America had to offer, would find some novelty in hosting a real-life Greek in their home away from home.

After I knocked for a few minutes, a bleary-eyed, tussle-haired, shirtless chap answered the door slowly. I greeted him cheerfully—perhaps too cheerfully—and he cringed at the sound of my voice. He shut the door without responding.

I was undaunted. These were fraternity houses, after all! *Fraternity!* Brotherhood, connection, family even! In the spirit of the fraternity of all humanity I would find a meal, I was sure of it. And if I was lucky, a place to crash for the night. I knocked on the next house down the row.

"Oh, man, I'd love to help but we have, like, this problem."

"What's the problem?"

"Well, you know, the brawl and all."

I did not know. "The brawl and all?"

"You know, last night. Seventeen of us arrested. Police came and all that. It was kinda crazy."

"So there are a lot of empty beds then?"

"Oh, no, everybody's back. Well, everybody 'cept Jonah, who's still in the hospital. There's some plan for payback tonight. And since we're sort of under investigation at the moment, it's, you know, probably not, like, the best time."

"No, doesn't sound like it. Well, good luck with the, you know, payback and all."

"Yeah, man, should be sweet."

Four more houses and no better luck. Bruised, dazed boys at the door, or no answers at all. I was a bit shocked: Where was the legendary southern hospitality and university-style thirst for learning? How many times did a stranded Englishman ask them for some kindness? I was beginning to feel sorry for myself.

Once the downward slope of self-pity begins, it can be devilishly difficult to interrupt. Soon I found myself in a very dark place. The whole world is against me, I imagined; nothing will ever work out. It amounts to self-sabotage, I know, but that doesn't mean I'm able to stop the damage: I retreat to my shell and ignore the world. I fill my head with stories of how everything that can go wrong will. I looked at the high afternoon sun, convinced—when it was barely mid-afternoon—that I'd be sleeping on the streets tonight. It was hopeless.

I imagined myself back in London, my flat awaiting me; the fridge full and the take-out menus on the counter. Food and lodging and *money* and ease. Would I prefer that? I asked myself. It was easier, yes. But it wasn't life. I remembered the evening in my flat, with Che on the screen, and his mission becoming mine.

"I'd rather be here," I said aloud to no one. It was true. I would rather be here. The cycle of self-pity was broken. Whatever small or large situation we find ourselves in, there is always a solution. We always have choices, even when we feel that we don't.

I reached the end of Frat Row, and turned to face the imposing houses.

Strutting up to the next house, this time I didn't knock. I waltzed right in and greeted a group of guys playing Ping-Pong in their recreation room.

"Gentlemen, I'm a Brit traveling America in search of kindness and beer. Have you any to offer?"

Eight guys turned my way, the only sound the ping-pong ball falling from the table and bouncing across the room.

"Well, we've always got beer. But foreigners don't drink for free," one of the guys smiled. "I'm Brett, president of our lovely fraternity." He stuck out his hand.

So these guys at least appreciated courage. "I'm Leon. I'm headed from Times Square to the Hollywood sign with no food, no car, no lodging, and nothing but the crazy idea that Americans will help me if I ask. If the beer's not free for me, then I wonder what you'll make me do if I tell you what I really want."

"What's that?" Brett asked.

"For you guys to buy me a ticket to my next stop."

"And where's your next stop?"

"Wherever you say, as long as it gets me closer to California."

Brett looked around at his friends. "Aaron," he called out. "Go get Brandon. Tonight's not gonna be such a drag after all." He slapped me on the shoulder and laughed, and the others joined in. I chuckled, happy to have found a responsive group, but more than somewhat nervous about what they might have planned.

"Here you go, Leon." He tossed me a paddle. "Best of five."

The rest of the afternoon was spent in preparation. The kegs came around the side of the house, loaded in the back of a pickup truck. The girls started showing up around five p.m., their jeans cut off high on their hips, and their makeup a work of art. The music started playing as the sun hid behind the house across the street. I'd lost more games of Ping-Pong than I could count, continued to say phrases with my British accent to the giggling delight of the sorority girls, their boyfriends' arms dangling over their shoulders, and eaten half a bag of pretzels and a few too many Fig Newtons.

"So, everybody!" Brett yelled at the gathered crowd. "This here is Mr. Leon from across the pond. He's on his way to California, and needs our help. I told him the brothers here were happy to oblige, but we'd like a little something in return." The crowd cheered. He looked down at me from the chair he was standing on. "Leon, my friend, I hope you're up for an adventure."

"I am afraid of nothing!" I said to cheers and whoops. Perhaps the most blatant lie I have ever told. I was caught up in the energy of the place. "I will go anywhere, do anything, sell my body (though I'm sure there'll be few takers) and soul! If you let me stay with you and send me on my way!" The volume of the crowd spiked. I was enjoying myself.

"Let me prove my manliness!" I continued, pulled along by the testosterone in the room, "and my legendry platinum cojones!"

"Shall we let him prove his platinum cojones?" Brett asked the crowd. They responded in one resounding voice: "YES!"

"Then what shall it be?"

A thousand voices—or so it seemed—shouted ideas.

"Drink a keg of beer!"

"Jump from the roof to the pool!"

"Take a piss on the University President's porch!"

"Steal a campus police car!"

And then one voice emerged. As soon as it spoke, I knew it would win out. It was meant to be:

"Run naked to kiss Homer's ass!"

The gathered mass of students went crazy.

"It is decided then," proclaimed Brett, still poised upon his chair. "You shall run naked across the campus of our fine university, and kiss the naked ass of the statue of Homer. And if you complete this feat of daring and manliness, then you shall have a bed, free beer, and a ticket to. . . . Where shall we send him?"

"How much money we got!" someone asked. "Who's in?"

A hat got passed around, and ones and change began to weigh it down. I'd have been touched if I thought the donations were prompted by caring for me; in truth, they just wanted to see a man run naked down the road. I couldn't blame them.

"Thirty-three dollars!" Daniel, Brett's friend, hollered when he finished counting.

"Excellent! You shall streak to Homer, kiss his butt, and return without being caught by the police. If you pull this off we will put you up for the night and buy you a ticket to as far as we can get you for thirty-three bucks. If you don't, you're on your own!" Brett determined.

I had not been given much of an option. "But . . ." I stammered. "If they catch me they will bloody deport me!"

"Whoa," said a somewhat drunk underclassman. "I've never seen someone deported."

"I'm sure it's not that entertaining," I replied. I wondered if this had possibly gone too far. I could see the headlines now: "Crazy Brit Arrested for Streaking at U.V.A." Then I saw my father's disapproving face. These were frat guys, after all, notorious for embarking on shocking stunts and life-threatening risks. Was I up to their measure of adventure?

Every fiber of my body was telling me this was a bad idea. I did not travel all this way to suffer the ignominy of being carted off to jail with only a towel around my waist. And yet . . . if I agreed to play along with this stunt I knew they'd keep their end of the bargain, and I'd have a roof over my head for the night and a ticket to my next destination.

My old life was spent behind a desk doing things that evoked absolutely no inspiration in me. I was perpetually bored in a life devoid of adventure. And here I was being offered a chance to experience the rush of life, and the thrill of a group of people cheering me on. One of the desires behind this experiment of mine was to experience life at its fullest, and if that meant running across a rotunda naked then this was what I was going to do. I had lived below the radar for years, here was a light-hearted way to stand out and reclaim a sense of joy that I had extinguished for so many years. I was going to run naked. I was going to leave behind not just my clothes but my old self, the baggage that hindered me. It would be a beautiful thing. Sort of.

"Whaddaya say, Leon?" asked Brett.

I waited, the crowd eager for my reply.

"I'll do it!" The room erupted in applause. "C'mon!" I yelled over them, joining Brett on a chair. "Is anyone going to indulge in this lunacy with me? There'll be far more incentive to actually go ahead with this if I'm running against an opponent. Anyone?"

The crowd pushed a thin, blond-haired guy toward me. "Todd's up for anything," a big guy in a football jersey said. "In fact, he's a really fast runner and ready to crush you. You'll go with him, right, Todd?"

"Only if I can wear my Superman cape!" Todd grinned.

This was getting more surreal by the second. Now I had to race the man of steel himself.

"One caveat," I said, calming the crowd. "I cannot risk being deported. I'll run naked, but . . ." I paused for dramatic effect. "If he gets to wear a cape, I get to put my boxers back on if I see any official looking person! If the police arrive, I'll slip them on and stay in the country. Deal?"

Brett convened an impromptu meeting of the heads of the frat house and I awaited my fate. Having a roof over my head lay in the balance.

"Okay! Boxer shorts in hand! Agreed!" several said in unison as they emerged from their summit.

The crowd poured out the door, blue plastic cups in each of their hands. They gathered on the front lawn in a circle, Todd and I in the middle.

"You ready, man?" he asked.

"To run naked across U.V.A. on a beautiful summer evening? You bet I am!" I was never so thankful for a moonless night.

"To the rotunda!" said someone in the crowd. The

group walked en masse down the street, a noise and laughter machine moving through the Charlottesville night. We reached the famed rotunda, designed by Jefferson himself, who no doubt erected his noble monument for just such a time as this.

"Okay, boys!" Brett bellowed. "Get naked!"

Todd was faster at undressing than any man I've ever seen. His clothes were in a pile on the grass before my shirt and shoes were off. He donned his Superman cape as I placed my pants on the lawn, crumpled up my boxers in my hand and watched the circle part in front of me.

"On the count of three . . ." said Brett.

My heart was pounding—I could hear it in my ears. My toes were wet in the grass, and the streetlights cast mean shadows across the road ahead.

"One . . ." said the crowd. "Two . . . *three!*"

We were off, Todd in his cape and me in my nothings, an odd couple if ever there was one. The man of steel and I eyed each other as we sprinted through the public square. It was freedom and joy and youth and life. I could actually feel the old Leon recede a little further, the new Leon loosened from his chains. To the students cheering behind us, this was merely another prank to enjoy until they moved onto the next one. For me it was a rite of passage, a break (literally) from the suit-wearing business man confined to an old method of existence. A surge of energy coursed through me. I was not going back to that old way of life. The old Leon was not going to reclaim me; it was time to keep running. I ran, and fast. It was time to live. It was time to change. What awaited me was anybody's guess, but right now it was about winning this damn race!

We streaked with all our might that night, and I reached

Homer mere seconds before my new superhero buddy. With a great smack I accomplished the feat I had set out to do—I kissed Homer on his bum and thus came as close to the classics as I ever would. I turned to run back to the starting point. I could see the crowd before me; their voices raised with their hands, a few girls perched upon the shoulders of their men. I bounded into them all, enveloped by cheering frat guys who promised to fill my belly with beer after my success.

I pulled my boxers on and shook Todd's hand.

"Your friends in England will be impressed when you tell them you raced Superman and won," he said.

"My friends in England won't believe any of this happened," I responded.

By the time we'd returned to the frat house—in higher spirits than when we had set off—word had spread of the unforgettable feat of the fearless Brit, and other guys from surrounding fraternities joined the party. Some of their faces I recognized from earlier in the day. The tussle-haired guy from the first house, the boy set on revenge from the second, the silent types from the third and fourth and fifth and sixth. They smiled and raised a glass, all of these bitter enemies in a room tonight, joined by the sense that fun was in the air, that something joyful had happened. Now they wanted to be a part. The "brawl and all" of the previous night was history. Tonight, we toasted the race and Homer's ass. I was soon cheered as an all-conquering hero, and between shots of Johnny Walker told the story of my quest to the men who had, hours before, turned me away.

"Well, Leon, that was one helluva race," said Brett. "You are one funny-looking naked man." The crowd agreed. "The beer and bed are yours; along with . . ." he reached in his pocket and pulled out the donation from the group. "A train ticket costing thirty-three dollars. While you're there, we ask only one thing."

"What is that?"

"That you run naked on the front lawn of the University of Charleston!" The crowd obviously found this appealing.

"If while there I can find a man with a Superman cape, I promise to run with him with my boxer shorts in hand."

"Fair enough," Brett smiled. Then he turned to the crowd, raising a blue plastic cup to the sky. "To Leon!"

"To Leon!" They echoed.

"A funny-looking naked Brit!"

"A funny-looking naked Brit!" the crowd roared.

A girl came up and hugged me, then kissed me on the cheek. "Good luck, Leon!" she said, as guys and girls slapped my shoulders and shook my hand. So this is the college life, I thought. Turns out it wasn't too late for me to find it after all.

5

Faith Opens a Thousand Doors

Faith is believing in things when
common sense tells you not to.

—George Seaton

"What did you say?" I couldn't believe my ears.

"John Wayne."

"That's your name."

"Yessir." He actually touched the tip of his hat. "Named after my grandfather."

It was early morning, and I was still groggy, half certain that the previous night's shenanigans were but a dream. Had I really stripped off all my clothes and sprinted naked through a small southern town, with a spindly Superman beside me? Daniel woke me up and made coffee and cereal, and I packed my light rucksack. For a few short hours I had become one of the brothers, and I would take that with me for a long time. I said farewell and headed to the train station, my eyes on Charleston, when I met up with a cabbie waiting in line outside the station.

"Beautiful morning," I said.

"It is that," he replied, looking up from his paper. "You certainly don't sound like you're from 'round here."

"No, I'm from England."

"Well, how about that. How's Charlottesville treatin' ya?"

"Can't complain!" I couldn't. "I'm Leon."

"John Wayne," he said, sticking out a wrinkled, suntanned hand. "Pleased to meet you."

"What did you say?"

"John Wayne."

"That's your name?"

"Yessir. Named after my granddaddy."

"He wasn't by chance . . ." I hoped he would take my meaning without my having to ask.

"The famous Wayne? Nah. But I used to pretend he was. Got me lots of girls in college back in the day!"

"I can imagine. Have any good stories to tell about such an interesting name?"

"Nah, nothing surprising. My life's not necessarily been full of too many surprises, if you know what I mean."

I nodded. I knew exactly.

"The biggest surprise prob'ly when my son hooked up over the Internet with a Swedish girl."

"Bet that doesn't happen much in Charlottesville."

"You'd make money on that bet. It doesn't happen never. But he met her in a chat room—you know a chat room?"

"I've heard."

"Yeah, and they fell in love, so he went over there. Turns out, though, she wasn't Swedish at all. She was from New York. And he wasn't Swedish of course. He was Virginian, you know, American through and through. But they neither one knew it 'cause they were, you know, speaking in the language . . ."

"They were speaking Swedish to each other."

"Right, right. They both thought they were gonna meet somebody exotic and all, and then he shows up and they realize they're just two regular old Americans who happen to know Swedish."

"How'd that work out?"

"Oh, it didn't. He was back here 'fore long. Married a good girl from Richmond. Which suits me fine. Richmond's closer than Stockholm anyway."

"So a happy ending."

"I suppose so! Here's a picture of their little one . . ."

The announcer at the station called my train, and I bade farewell to Mr. John Wayne, and pondered how often life trips us up. It appears to pull us one way, and when we arrive, it's often not what we expect. I was learning slowly to adjust my own expectation of every day, of every conversation, and to embrace the unpredictability of it all as a joy and a virtue. Who knew what might come next? And who would want to?

I hopped on the afternoon train to Charleston, West Virginia, and thought about all the characters I'd met so far. I call them characters, because that's exactly what they are: figures in a larger story. From my perspective, as the main character of my own story, they are supporting cast; they enter and exit, leaving behind a mark or a thought or a memory. But what I was learning was profound: they didn't just add to the story. They *were* the story. I simply had no story without them. Each person I met along the way was contributing something of themselves to my odyssey. The roles they played composed my own narrative, and without their moving in my life, that narrative collapsed, and I would be left alone, just as before, with no story worth telling. The inverse was equally as compelling: I was a bit character in someone else's epic, too. I was helping to build the narrative of every person I met. The frat boys in my story had given me a chance to open myself to joy, and I had given them a memory, too. Their own stories were larger because of our time together. Each of our stories expands when we enter each other's lives.

On the train from Charlottesville to Charleston, mine was about to become much larger.

Gene Adams was old and wrinkly. He had a deep, gravelly voice, and a sparkle in his eye that suggested a much younger man lived inside this body.

"I'm an avid train traveler," he said proudly. "It's my favorite way to get from A to B."

Traveling by train, he explained, enabled him to connect with people in a way that plane travel did not.

"Why, do you think?"

"Simple: on a plane, you're moving too fast."

Here's Gene's explanation: the speed of travel is inversely related to the ability to connect. That is, he says, the "arithmetic of travel."

"We used to walk places, although you probably don't remember this. But we did. We'd walk to school, walk to work, walk to church, walk to see friends and family. And what did we do while we walked? We talked with each other. We joked and laughed and caught up on the day. Sometimes we'd take a horse and buggy—I'm serious, that's how old I am! And what did we do? We talked then, too. Even played games. But we got to our destination faster on horses and buggies. Thus, less time to talk. Then we started taking trains, and we got there even faster. Then cars, and we got their faster, now planes, the fastest of all, until they come up with something new and speedier.

"And all along the way, we have connected less and less; talked less and less. Now, we don't talk at all. We don't see the point. Now, the journeys are just about speed—getting someplace as fast as possible. Efficiency is the enemy of connection."

Gene had a voice you could listen to all day. "So," I asked him, "you take the train to—"

"To slow things down," he said with a smile. "I can't walk everywhere, of course—I can't be that much of a rebel. Besides, these old legs won't do me much good. But I can take a train. I can say to the world, I choose to take a slower route, to take more time to get from A to B, and while I'm doing that, while I'm *not* taking the fastest route, I'm going to take the time to meet some folks who are taking their time, too."

I grew silent, thinking of the number of times I had actually spoken to anyone on a plane. It wasn't very many. Any time someone tried, I'd answer curtly and stick my nose self-importantly into a book I wasn't really reading. Sitting in a metal tube for hours with a mass of humanity, I would meet *no one*. I would exit the plane with my story as small as it had been when I boarded.

Yes, Gene was right. And he was a living example of his philosophy. Here I was with a wise old man learning lessons about life that seemed to have passed me by.

"You have to ask yourself," he said, looking out the window. "Why spend so much time trying to get somewhere, when you aren't even enjoying the journey?"

I smiled. He had me.

"For instance," he said. "I haven't asked you where you're going, have I?"

"Oh, I'm headed—"

"Oh no, don't tell me!" he said with a chuckle. "That's where the trouble starts. We talk only of where we're going, where we're heading, what we've got to do when we get there. All the space and the miles and minutes between become an obstacle to leap over. Instead, I think the destination is the obstacle; it draws such attention from us that we aren't allowed to think about what happens in the middle, between here and there."

"He's talking your ear off, isn't he?" An older woman sat down next to Gene, her trousers carefully ironed, and her pearls shimmering. "I'm Lucy, Gene's wife. Don't worry, I've heard it all before, too."

"Your husband's a wise man," I said. And I meant it.

"Oh, I just steal all my best ideas from her," he said, and kissed her on the cheek.

"How long have you been married?" I asked, acknowledging their rings, which looked delightfully old-fashioned.

"Fifty-two years next April," Gene said.

"Congratulations," I offered. "That's quite an accomplishment."

"Yes, well, Gene won't call it an accomplishment. He says that makes it sound—"

"Like it's over!" he said. "Like we've done it and it's finished. But it's not!" he said with a finger raised in the air. "It continues!"

Gene and Lucy, I later learned, were on their way to Indianapolis. The more we talked, the more I felt inspired by this simple but profound couple, they had been married for over a half a century. They were pleasant, well-informed, engaging. They seemed to find me trustworthy, too. After our initial chat, Gene offered to call friends of his in Charleston who might let me stay with them. I might already have a place to stay—and I hadn't even asked.

By the time we were approaching the Appalachians, slowly making our way around the bends and valleys, Gene had become my hero. The man was smart, no question, but the guy was literally a walking history book. He'd been personally involved in two of the most powerful moments of the twentieth century: as a naval officer, he had taken part in the 1962 Cuban naval blockade, physically present at the zenith of the Cold War. As an engineer with NASA, he had worked on the Apollo missions that took Neil Armstrong and his fellow astronauts to the moon and those after Armstrong to the outer reaches of space. Gene must have seen my boyish glee upon hearing his stories.

"Let me guess: you wanted to be an astronaut when you were little."

I shook my head. "Even then I knew that wasn't possible for me. I just wanted to watch them. I still think of them. Whenever I am at a low point I often think of how Neil Armstrong landed on the moon. Humans landed on the moon! I mean, this is absolutely unbelievable. Only a few decades before, man had learned how to fly! Anyway, I think to myself, if Neil Armstrong could walk on the moon then anything is possible. And I mean *anything*."

"Leon, my friend, you get it. That's exactly what the

moon landing was supposed to mean for all of us. It's *all* possible."

I smiled. Gene was just an old man on a train. But start talking to somebody—*anybody*—and an entire world can emerge.

The high mountains of West Virginia emerged, too, and their height and trees meant limited cell phone coverage, thus no way to contact Gene and Lucy's friends. "Why don't you continue on with us to Indianapolis? You can use our son's old room." Lucy offered as we entered Charleston.

I smiled sadly. "I wish I could, but I cannot. My ticket only takes me this far."

"Well, if you're ever in the area . . ." Gene handed me his card. I took it gratefully, said good-bye to them both and stepped out into the dark West Virginia night.

I arrived in Charleston at about ten p.m. to a familiar site: deserted streets. Hotels with their lights off, no one at their desks. Streetlights flickering and threatening to fade and leave me in the black of night. Three hotel rejections—and not one real moment of despair—later, I found my good Samaritan: a late-night hotel manager offered me a room at her hotel on the condition that I would leave early the next morning so that she would not be found out.

"It's against policy," she whispered, looking both ways. "But you look really tired, and it is dark as hell out there . . ."

She was right. It was dark as hell out there. But the room she gave me was heaven. My first night in a four-star hotel, I didn't want to sleep: I wanted to jump on the bed, watch television, and stare out the window at the river that gracefully winds its way through Charleston.

But I slept for a few hours, got up early, and quietly left my key at the lobby desk—no one was in sight and I sighed relief that my friend the night manager's job was safe. I turned to the continental breakfast, to perform my usual binge, and was in the middle of gulping down a full jug of orange juice when a small voice spoke from near the pastries.

"Wow."

I quickly put the jug on the table and wiped my mouth. A short, young brunette woman—or girl, as she didn't look much over eighteen—was laughing at me. "Sorry?"

"I've just never seen anyone drink orange juice that fast—or that much of it!"

"Oh, well, you know. I need my vitamin C. Healthy bones and all that."

"And what about the five doughnuts? Those full of vitamins, too?" She smiled.

"Of course! Loaded with 'em! Growing boys like me need our carbs!"

She chuckled and so did I. Thinking it better to leave before she asked what room I'd stayed in, I quickly finished up and said a hasty good-bye, flinging my rucksack over my shoulder and heading out to the mountain town of Charleston.

The river sliced the city in half, and I headed first to the bridge, to see both sides of the town, and peer at the mountains that loom over the buildings. Nestled in this valley, Charleston has somewhat the feeling of a Swiss village. Until you hear the citizens speak. They all have a friendly southern twang, a soft lilt in their speech that makes you want to sit across a table from them and play checkers.

My instincts must have been right, because in downtown Charleston nearly every shop sells checkerboards, and I saw old men sitting out front, dueling dispassionately across a table. I window-shopped a bit, looking at the arts and crafts and homemade sweets, torturing myself with things that I could not afford. At lunchtime, I popped into a typical American diner, where a couple of servers were taking care of a handful of customers.

"How many?" she asked, reaching for menus.

"How many what?"

"For lunch. Is anyone joining you?"

"I don't think so."

She gave me a funny smile, not sure if I was trying to be clever, and I followed her to a table.

"Sorry," I said, "but I'm rather short of cash. Can I wash dishes to earn my lunch?"

The girl had long dark hair pulled into a ponytail and oozed southern charm.

"I don't have the authority to hire you, but you can talk to our manager."

In my experience, it never helps to talk to a manager, but she was already calling for him before I could object.

"Where y'all from?" she asked, motioning me to a booth and heading to the kitchen for her boss.

"Across the pond," I offered, and she laughed at that before disappearing into the open doorway.

"Which pond?" she peered back at me.

"The Atlantic."

"Ha. Everybody knows that's an ocean, silly."

A few minutes later she returned. "Sorry, we can't let you work here without going through all the channels."

"Which channels?" I asked.

"The . . . proper ones?" she said, as though it might be a question. I thanked her and took a few mints from the jar by the cash register, and headed back toward the train station. The day was wearing on, my mind was asking what was next, and my head was feeling hot—the sun was baking my bald British head. I passed a wall-hangings store and peered at myself in a mirror. My head looked like a large red mango. I needed shade, or better yet, a hat.

I passed my hotel, and saw the funny girl from that morning who had watched me—and laughed at me—as I gulped the orange juice. She saw me too, and I waved from outside. When she waved back, I took the chance.

Stepping through the automatic doors, I felt the cool air conditioning pour over my face.

"Hello again," she said, with a small smile. "Quite a suntan you're working on there."

"Yes, well, thank you for noticing. I wonder if you have any suntan lotion?"

"Sure, of course. In the gift shop. To your left."

"Well, thank you, but, there's a bit of a problem . . ." She looked at me curiously. "You see, I don't exactly have . . . any money. I mean, I do; I have five dollars. But it's all I get for the day, you see?"

"Your parents still handing out your allowance?"

"Um, kind of. My producer, actually. You see . . ." I paused. Should I take the chance? "Would you like to hear a story?"

As expected, she did.

"You're brave," she said, after having listened patiently to my story, which was getting quite good, I must say. "I'd like to help. Where you goin' next?"

"Well, west. But who knows? What do you suggest?"

"How about Lexington?"

"Lots of nice horse country around there," she added. "Do you ride?"

"Not in years," I said. "But I may have to if I can't get a hitch to Hollywood."

She laughed. "My shift ends at three. Hang around in the lounge, and when I'm off, we'll figure out a plan."

"Perfect."

"There's some orange juice in the fridge behind the counter, if you want it. Vitamin C and all that."

At three o'clock promptly, we left the hotel together.

"Where we headed?" I asked.

"Well, I need you to meet my mom."

"Oh, well it seems a little soon . . ."

"Ha! Yes, well, I want her to meet you so she'll know I'm safe, you know, if I'm going to take you to Lexington."

I was stunned. "Wait—you're going to drive me there?"

"Why not?"

"Brilliant! Now, I do want to meet your mother! And your father—I need to ask for your hand in marriage!"

Ashley's mother was a forty-year-old version of Ashley herself; as friendly as her daughter; and she, for some odd reason, trusted me with her daughter. Ashley drove me to the mall, and we walked around a little before she bought me a feast of fajitas. Minutes later we were in her car, breezing down the highway. I felt blessed with luck—or maybe by something else? It turned out that Ashley was a devout Christian, which she pronounced a few minutes after we'd hit the freeway. As I was a dedicated agnostic, someone who could just not bring himself to believe that there was a man sitting in the clouds overlooking everyone yet, at the same time, someone also who could not quite disbelieve that there was a powerful energy or force that was beyond my understanding. I was glad for the ride, and for the good company, but a little fearful that I was about to undergo a conversion attempt.

I have never felt a deep connection with God, or a God-presence. I don't dislike the idea, or people who find the idea so appealing as to talk about it a lot. It's just never been me. But my version of me was changing those days. So when Ashley started talking, I decided there was little risk in listening.

"God is real, and God is capable of doing things. I can't touch him and give him a hug, but he's there," she started. "You don't see God, after all. I mean, I've never seen him."

"You just pretend he's there, yeah?"

"No. He *is* there. But this is where it gets fuzzy. You know the wind's there, right?"

"Yeah."

"Do you see the wind?"

"No."

"You see the effects of the wind."

"Yeah."

She was actually beginning to make sense now.

"But I see him change my mother's life—" she paused, her voice broken and her eyes wet. "Sorry!" She smiled, taking a moment to swallow and compose herself. "I see him change my sister's life, I see him change people around me. I see very tangible happenings."

"Like what?"

"Well, my mom was very ill. It was bad. It was bad for quite a while. And at the same time my sister was really struggling. She was angry, I think, and got into some bad stuff, with bad people—you know how it is: small town, small minds, blah, blah, blah. And for a while, it looked like my whole family was going to disappear. My mom was going to die, and my sister, too, probably, if she kept living that way. The only good thing that came out of it was that I learned to pray. I prayed so hard. For both of them."

"What happened?"

"Everything changed. I mean, not right away. But my mom got better. Not like a stupid miracle or anything. But I am certain God was helping. And then she came home from the hospital, and my sister was there, and for the first time in a long time, we were all together, eating dinner, watching TV, and I could see it in my sister's face: she didn't want the other life. She wanted this life. With us. Safe. And she started changing, too. That took longer—and took a lot of prayer and patience!" Ashley laughed. "But she changed all right. And now, I still sometimes can't believe it, but we're all fine. We're doing fine."

Everybody's known crazy religious people. I see them mainly on the tube these days, but others know them intimately. But something different is going on with people like Ashley. Something wonderful. I was truly touched by this young girl's understanding of how a force that's not of this world somehow affects her life and the lives of those closest to her. It seemed that she had gained a tremendous inner strength from the belief in a presence greater than herself.

But America's a funny place. The good kind of spiritual discussion so easily becomes the bad kind. The role of religion in American society has always been paradoxical and mixed up. Experts can hardly describe it with ease or specificity, much less young girls in middle America. But something about Ashley was making me think.

"Why is it," I asked her, "that when I watch the news, when I watch religious channels, people don't explain it the way you've explained it? I mean, the way you've explained it just now makes a lot more sense than these preachers who are screaming about how the devil is coming to get you. . . . You know, he's going to eat you and he's gonna—"

"What you're talking about is fire and brimstone. That reaches some people. In my circle of life, it doesn't reach many; it just scares them. I don't want to live scared. I want to live abundantly, joyously, and happy to walk with God, *not* in fear of him. Believe it or not, I can't talk to most people like this. Sometimes you need a stranger."

"I know exactly how you feel," I told her. "Trust me. I have faith. Never felt religious, really, but I'll say it again, it's the first time anybody has talked to me about religion . . ."

"This is why I believe in God. You know. I hear about your trip, and initially, I wonder what it is, why I care. You know, coming on this trip sounds cool; I want to be a part of that. But I've thought about it today, prayed about it, called my mother. It was not an easy choice for me. But I felt I should, you know? That maybe I needed to talk to you about this. That maybe *you* needed to talk about this."

I looked out the window at the wind blowing across a wheat field. "I know exactly what you mean."

The moment touched me. Here I was with a complete stranger tackling the complexities of God. She had hit a nerve, she had connected with me, and I felt that I had connected with her. Two strangers driving down the freeway, invoking the age-old emotion of humanity. Tears were by this time streaming down her face and I was close to tears myself. Her explanation of the way that God had changed lives in her family couldn't be ignored.

After a bit of time, we pulled over at a rest area and switched places. It was fantastic being at the wheel. I was struck by how readily Ash—by now I was calling her by the shorter version of her name, as she told me I should—trusted me. Was it because of her trust in people, faith in God, or my innocent appearance?

It was impossible to know at this early stage, but one thing was clear: trust was becoming a theme of my trip—not just the trust that I had to have for people, but the trust that they had to have for me as well. They had no idea who I was. Rationally it would have been far easier to ignore my requests for help, yet something was telling them that spending time with me was the correct thing to do. They had bypassed the initial fear that was completely understandable. They made the conscious decision to veer away from what they had been told by society and found a way to help a stranger. To help someone who needed a helping hand.

We reached Lexington sooner than I'd hoped. On the outskirts I pulled over to let her drive, since she knew the town. Before going too deep into the city, she found one of the nicest motels in sight and registered a room for me, paying the bill in advance.

When I had settled into the room, we went on a car ride around the town and stopped off at a service station. I wandered into the gift shop.

"I have a gift for you."

"You have a gift for me?" she sounded surprised.

"A few gifts, actually . . ."

"A few!" she said with a smile.

"This is a 'thank you' for everything that you did today."

"Isn't that sweet, thank you."

From the convenience store's plastic bag, I pulled out a

tooth brush as Ashley had complained earlier about forgetting all her toiletries. "This is a tooth brush," I said, stating the obvious.

"Yay, a tooth brush!" she said gleefully.

"Because it was all I could afford. Not because you have bad breath."

"Right. Got it."

"And this is a one-dollar scratch card."

"Oh, awesome!"

"This is another one-dollar scratch card."

"Oh, thank you so much!"

"And because I'm not allowed to have any money at the end of the night, this is all the money I have left and it's to pay for the motel room." It was about twenty-seven cents—the cheapest motel room on earth!

She took the change and held it to her chest dramatically. "And I have a gift for you," she said, reaching behind the seat.

"I think you've given me enough—"

She handed me a small box of orange juice. "I stole it from the hotel," she said. "Because you know, growing boys need their vitamin C."

She smiled and I gave her a long hug.

"Thanks, Ash."

"God bless you, Leon."

She gave me a peck on the cheek, and I shut the car door behind me. My steps felt lighter. Riding the elevator up to the motel room, I looked at myself in the mirror. I'd covered only a couple hundred miles this day, but it didn't matter. I smiled at my sunburned head. I'd found joy in the journey; the destination would come soon enough. Gene, I thought, would be proud.

6
Crossroads

The pessimist sees difficulty in every opportunity.
The optimist sees the opportunity in every difficulty.

—*Winston Churchill*

When I look back on my time traveling across America, I don't remember much of Nick, my producer. No offense to him; I'm sure he did a great job and made the whole Englishman-travels-America-looking-for-kindness project work as a television show. But he was mostly invisible to me, part of the backdrop, never really on stage. And that may have been his best work: he let me live my story, and never got in the way of the happenstance that made magic of my itinerant days.

Except for one moment.

I had found my way to a nearby truck stop which seemed

alive with activity—a promising place to find a friend and a ride.

Before I could turn my attention to the trucks lined up in front of me like a slumbering army, Nick was running toward me, cell phone in hand. His face drawn, and paler than usual.

He held out his arm, pushing the phone toward me. It was strange to be handed the phone, a forbidden aspect of my journey, and an odd reminder of my previous life. I say previous life because I was already swimming as far away from that existence as possible. The phone seemed unfamiliar already, like finding a wallet you used when you were a kid, or seeing someone else's shoes neatly placed outside your front door.

"It's your mother," he panted. "Seems urgent."

I grabbed the phone and put it to my ear. "Mama? What's going on?"

"Leon! I've been trying your cell but you never pick up!"

"I don't have my phone, Mama, remember? Part of the experience—"

"Yes, yes, but listen, Leon . . ." She was being very serious, I could hear it in her tone. "I have the test results here, and—"

So, I had been feeling sick for the past year, unable to sleep properly, suffering from constant headaches; I had even fainted a couple of times. It was, I thought, all part of my disconnected life—too much to do, too little time, no one to watch out for me or take care of me, no time to meet anyone who might. But that was all an excuse, I know. I wasn't ready for a relationship, wasn't really ready to be a friend or have a friendship of any value. The busy lifestyle may have given me an excuse, but I was hiding behind that busyness, avoiding placing myself in a vulnerable state, avoiding having to trust anyone. So I had been alone, and getting sicker. Discomfort was my lifestyle. The physical trouble was likely a manifestation of a spiritual and emotional illness, I thought. Fix the inside, fix the outside.

Turns out it might be a little more complicated than that.

"—your blood sugar is high, Leon. Very high. And the doctor's not at all pleased with the idea of you going days without knowing what you're eating or drinking, or where you're sleeping. And frankly, neither am I."

"Mama, I'm fine.

"Yes, well, I don't believe you, and I don't remember you telling me you were sick when you started this ridiculous journey—"

"Now you're sounding exactly like Dad."

"Well he's not wrong all the time! Listen, Leon . . ."

That was the sign. *Listen, Leon* was the set-up. The punch line was next.

"I want you to come home. And I want you to come home *now.*"

I didn't reply.

"Leon, listen . . ." (The inversion of *Listen, Leon* was just as powerful.) "This is not a discussion. You play whatever games you like with your life, but when it comes to your health, you listen to me. Tell your friends, that you'll need to get to an airport—where did say you were?"

"Lexington. That's in Kentucky."

"Oh, well, I'm sure it's lovely there, but are you close to a large city with—"

"Mama!"

"—an international airport? Oh, I wish I knew American geography better. How about—"

"Mama!"

"Washington? Is that close to Washington? They have daily flights to London—"

"Mama!!"

"Yes?"

"I love you. But I am not coming home. It is completely out of the question. End of story."

"Listen, Leon—"

Not this time. "No, Mama."

"You can continue the trip when you're well!"

She was pleading with me now, and I must admit to feeling touched. But I was no longer her little boy gallivanting in the back garden, running from his brothers, retreating into her kitchen for protection and food. More to the point I was no longer the Leon of her recent memory either.

"No, it has to happen now. This trip is—" The trip is what? I didn't know what to say. It was . . . "Everything," I said.

Everything. It was all I had. The only thing I had done with my life so far that even resembled a raison d'etre. This wasn't a trip. This was my life.

And I was *not* going home.

My mother is Greek and fiercely protective of all her children. I find that the Mediterranean blood coursing through her veins could at times inspire her to hysteria. Her motto: it's better to be safe than sorry!

I'd lived my life safe, and I felt more sorry about that than anything else.

"At least," she offered one last plea, "talk to the doctor. Just five minutes. I have his number . . ."

And so I did. Seated on the sidewalk in front of the wilting grass of the truck stop's convenience store, I called my doc in London.

I was hoping he'd be on leave, or attending to a medical emergency, totally unreachable. My mother seemed adamant that I was on the verge of serious irreversible illness unless I returned; surely this guy would be less hysterical. I wasn't so lucky. He picked up immediately, and after two minutes on the phone with him, it soon became evident the test results were indeed serious.

"In my professional opinion," he stated soberly, "you should stop what you are doing and return home. You're on the verge of diabetes. An immediate adjustment to a regular, scheduled diet and a prescription medical regime is necessary."

"But," I said softly, "I haven't yet reached the irreversible stage of being a diabetic, right?"

The doctor paused a moment. "No," he said. "But you are dangerously close."

"Well, better dangerous than sorry."

"Excuse me?"

"Nothing. Thanks, doc. I'll see you when I get back."

"And when will that be?"

"Dunno. Sometime soon after I touch the Hollywood sign. I'll take a picture for you."

I hung up and flipped the phone over to Nick.

"Well . . ." he said. "Are we, you know, heading back?"

I didn't answer him. At that moment a gentleman emerged from the convenience store with a cylinder of Pringles and a Diet Coke in his hand, and I stepped quickly to intercept him.

"Hello there!" I said cheerily. "Where you headed?"

"Indiana."

"Indiana! Great! Want some company?"

I looked back at Nick, who smiled. He ran back to gather the crew.

Indianapolis happened to be the home of Gene Adams. And in my right back pocket was his number. "If you're ever in the area . . ." This could be a very good day.

But first I'd have to get there with a truck driver named Chris, who was, well, a silent, reserved type, something you can easily become with seventy hours a week spent in the cab of your truck—or eighty hours a week enslaved in the world of finance in London. It was proving hard to get more than two words at a time out of him.

I looked over at him and tried to find some common ground: I sensed his solitary nature and hoped that our journey would break him out of his shell.

"You always been a truck driver?" I asked.

"Not always."

"What did you do before you hit the road?"

"Department of Corrections. For a while."

"Corrections department?"

"Prison. I was a guard."

"Wow. What kind of prison?"

"Maximum security. Wisconsin."

"Wow again. So that's where the really bad guys go, huh? Did you have any famous prisoners in there? Or infamous."

"Jeffrey Dahmer."

"*The* Jeffrey Dahmer?"

"Yup, killed just after I got there."

"Oh, right. Who killed him?"

"Prisoner."

"But why? I mean, the guy's in jail, right?"

"I always heard it was a gang hit. Issued from the outside. This gang from Milwaukee found somebody who was in prison who had life already, had no hope of getting out, and told him that they would take care of him and his family if he did this and he did it."

And just like that, the floodgates opened. For the next hour we talked about prisons. And when I say "we" I mean "he." Chris had a voice after all. We'd hit the gold mine, and the man was bringing up treasures at every turn. Stories of crazy days and old friends. It takes a certain kind of person to be a prison guard, he explained. A certain psychological state must be reached to deal with those society has deemed inappropriate for daily interaction with the rest of us.

An interesting fact Chris told me was that the United States, at any given moment, has 2.5 million of its citizens in prison. Misdemeanors. Felonies. Civil violations. Criminal offenses. Theft. Assault. Murder. And all of them are looked after by men and women like Chris, who interact daily with people who stare at the consequences of a life poorly lived, a life that led to prison.

"Whenever a prisoner got paroled, we'd give him his stuff, you know, that we got when he arrived. Kept all that crap filed away in a big storage room. But we'd always toss a new cigar in with the stuff. You know, as a way of saying congrats and wishing 'em the best. A couple of them walked out with that cigar between their teeth, sucking on their first taste of freedom."

"Freedom deserves at least a little celebration, right."

"Yeah," agreed Chris, then he looked somber. "Didn't happen very often."

Chris had met thousands of prisoners. For each of them condemnation had been granted by the state, but the government's not the only one with the power to incarcerate. I had in some way found myself in a prison of my own making, one to which I alone possessed the lock and the key. I had created this prison and had been sitting in it for years, telling myself constantly that I could not succeed and did not deserve success; a prison where I replayed negative aspects of my life over and over again; a prison where I was doomed to live out a life of mediocrity; a prison where I was destined to fail.

"Fuck that."

"Excuse me?"

"Oh, sorry." I'd spoken out loud. "No, I was just thinking to myself. You worked in cells, with guys locked inside, and now you're free. I was living a life that was constricted, like I was in a cell, and now I'm free, too. We are, I was thinking, far greater than the messages we tell ourselves."

Chris was silent for a moment. "Yes, I guess that's right." We stared out the windows for a moment. "Hey, you want some food?"

I turned to him, grinning. "Absolutely, I am starving."

Chris directed me to the small refrigerator and microwave behind the seats. I heated up some leftover chicken and steak with half a baked potato and some broccoli—acutely conscious of my new found need to eat healthy food.

Chris and I ate while the sun moved in and out of the clouds, and the radio played a mix of classic country and indie rock. It dawned on me, as I swallowed a bit of Diet Coke, that I was happy. In that moment, I couldn't imagine a place I'd rather have been. At first glance, Chris had appeared unapproachable and even dangerous, certainly not a candidate for friendship. We were as different as night and day, but for those few hours at least, more like brothers than strangers.

"Here's Indy," he said, the lights of the city looming ahead of us. "Any idea where you're headed?"

"Not really. But I have a phone number."

"Okay. Well, where do you want to get out?"

"Here's fine. Yeah, looks as good a place as any." It was dark, and I looked at a close-to-empty gas station and wondered if that was true; seemed there might be many places much better than this. "Is this a bad area?"

"Well, it's not . . . real nice, I wouldn't say. Here . . ." He rummaged through his console, a mess of papers and books, and pulled out a faded map. "This is a map of Indy. And we're, uh, we're somewhere . . . .yeah, right here." He pointed at a stretch of road just south of the city. "Take this with you, in case you get lost."

"Brilliant. Thanks." I pocketed the map, and scanned the dimly lit gas station. "Look, there's a phone booth. I'll just pop over there. But first . . ." I reached into my pocket, and handed him a cigar. "When we stopped for gas, I used $1.63 of my remaining money to buy you a parting gift. Chris, without you, I would be finished. So, thank you very, very much."

He looked at the cigar awkwardly.

"You know, because we're both out of our cells. Thought it was fitting."

"No, I get it." He turned it over in his hands. " . . . 'Cause freedom needs celebrating."

I smiled. "That's exactly right."

"Be safe, Leon."

"You, too, Chris."

As I waved farewell to Chris, I noticed a police car swerve from the inside lane toward the slow moving truck, lights and sirens blaring.

This did not look good.

The car skidded to a stop beside me, and the policeman got out with his right hand hovering at his gun holster.

I had heard the horror stories of American police: people being tasered for no reason, beatings on the side of the road, an apparent disregard for the rule of law. I never knew if these stories were true, and likely neither did the people telling them, but people outside the United States like to imagine that if the U.S. has one great flaw, it's that everybody gets to carry a gun, and too often those guns get fired, thus, the police have to be tough. I was concerned, especially since this particular police car decided to swerve in front of cars on the freeway in an attempt to get at me. He obviously wanted to speak with me. I assumed that it was not to welcome me to his state.

"What're you doing out here, boy!"

Boy? Bad start.

"I have just been given a lift and am on my way to the center of Indianapolis."

"You can't be serious." He chuckled a bit, but not in a way that implied I was being funny.

"I can't?"

"Downtown Indy at this hour? You can't be out here this time of day, don't you know that?"

"No sir, I was not aware of that actually."

"I should give you a citation for walking out here on the freeway."

"I am really sorry, I was just dropped off here by a friend and I am going to leave immediately."

"Do you realize what part of town you are in?" the officer said ominously.

"No, actually I am new to Indianapolis. Is this a good area?"

He laughed hard this time. "A good area? God, no. No it's not! I'd strongly suggest you find a cab and get out of this area quickly."

"Yes, officer, thanks. I wonder—"

Before I could ask for a ride, he was gone, lights flashing in the night.

The darkness was deep, and the traffic sparse. I'd gone from the safety of Chris's truck to a night that seemed to hold a good deal of uncertainty. The air chilled me.

I caught sight of the main road in the short distance, and climbed over a freeway fence into the glow of that great bastion of safety and American sanity, the local Burger King. I needed quarters for one of my dollar bills so I could call Mr. and Mrs. Adams. I also wanted the feeling of safety that only being in a group of people brought. While standing in line at the counter, a man who had followed me in from outside put his hand in his jacket and gave me what I am certain was a: "I am now going to kill you stare." Between Chris's ominous tone, the police officer's candid warning, the chill of the night air, and the depth of the darkness, I convinced myself that Indy would literally be the death of me.

I ducked into the bathroom, where a homeless man was washing himself in the sink, and quickly backed out. The man had gone, and so I moved as fast as possible to the check-out counter. I got my quarters while glancing nervously over my shoulder toward the door, and stepped cautiously into the night. I raced across the small parking lot toward the public phone to make the call to the Adams.

Someone was shouting in the distance, and a few lone figures moved beneath the streetlight. The phone rang.

"Pick up, pick up, pick up—*please* pick up."

I spun around, thinking I heard footsteps behind me.

"Pick up. Pick up—"

"Hello. Adams residence." Hearing Lucy's voice seemed like a small miracle.

"Mrs. Adams! Hi! This is Leon—we met on the train from Charlottesville to Charleston and your husband and I talked quite a while about the Cuban missile crisis and his role in the 1969 Apollo moon landings and the reason we travel and I know it is terribly late, but you said to call if—"

"Leon! Of course I remember you! What are you doing in town?"

"This is where the journey led me."

"The long and winding road that leads you to my door."

"Exactly!"

Our connection was immediate, but it was late, Mr. Adams was out of town, and I couldn't bet on a ride out to their place. But within five minutes Mrs. Adams had solved the problem: she booked me a hotel room in Indianapolis. Brilliant.

"The only drawback is that you'll have to get over to the other side of town."

"Oh, no problem. What's the fastest route?"

"You're not gonna like it," she warned.

"Try me."

"You'll have to go through downtown Indy, and well . . ."

"It's not a good place," I guessed. "Yeah, I gathered. But you know, I have my lucky streak going. I'll be fine!" I sounded cheery, but felt despair. Downtown Indy? This late? Yet, what other option did I have?

A hotel room awaited up ahead. Whatever surprises between now and then would be addressed as they came.

And surprises, there would be.

With the policeman's warning still reverberating, I started the long trek through downtown Indianapolis to my hotel. I was concerned about my safety, but told myself that I'd been fortunate thus far—why wouldn't the luck continue?

I saw four people moving toward me from between two dark buildings, and my heart beat quickly. I was contemplating my two options, hide or run, when I noticed that two of them were children, one no more than six years old. My nerves calmed a bit, thinking if it was safe for them to walk around, it was probably safe for me, too. If families could walk through Indy, then surely I could—especially if I stuck close to them. So I shouted a greeting.

"Good evening!"

They turned in unison, and slowed until I caught up with them. I saw them plainly now—a man and a woman who appeared to be husband and wife, and two children, a daughter maybe twelve or so, and a son of six or seven. I looked at them standing there, a few bags on their backs and in their hands, their coats buttoned. The two children were holding hands. So far, my trip had introduced me to individual Americans, but this was my first interaction with the American nuclear family. "Sorry to bother you all, but can you take a look at my map and tell me the safest way to get to the Marriot Hotel?" I made sure to emphasis the word "safest."

I noticed the father had a makeshift sling around his

shoulder. "Sorry, sir, but I don't know how to read," the man said, quickly followed by a similar comment by the woman.

I was stunned. "Oh . . . you're serious?" I probed.

"Absolutely, I never learned how to read," he said nonchalantly.

He looked to be in his early forties, living in the cradle of capitalism and prosperity. Yet he couldn't read. How could it be possible? I realized there was much illiteracy in places like Peru, Nepal, and other areas of the globe, but in America? It made no sense.

"Well, um. Where are you headed then?"

"Dunno exactly. Heard there was a free clinic in downtown. We're trying to find it, you know, my shoulder is really hurting."

I paid closer attention now, and it was clear that the man was in some discomfort. He had apparently dislocated his shoulder just hours before—I didn't ask how—and had been walking with his two children and wife for close to three hours searching for the clinic. They didn't have any money for a bus fare. And they had no health insurance. Both kids were wearing what could only be described as rags.

Rick was his name. His wife, Darby. His kids, Sean and Kendra.

"Can I walk with you?" I asked.

"Plenty of room on the road."

We walked, Rick limping a bit it seemed to me. And once again, I thought about the life I had left behind. A life of privilege and opportunity; a life that seemed so distant while I was exploring the vastness of America, yet one that I knew I would someday return to. The journey was an indulgence, a working out of personal matters and identity questions. My seeming poverty was chosen and entirely temporary. My reliance on the kindness of strangers was an experiment. If it didn't work out, I'd be poorer for it emotionally and spiritually, but I'd be able to return to a world of comfort. Yet here was a family of four, destitute and seemingly unable to pick themselves up from the crushing weight of poverty. Their's was an everyday existence absent of the freedom, security, and comfort that money brings. What to me was a temporary immersion was to this family a permanent reality. I felt like a fraud.

For most of my life, I have had a warped relationship with money. For years, most of my decisions were filtered through the prism of how much money I could make. This had been my driving force. My holy grail. Instead of pursuing the possibility of a profession that made my soul sing, I settled for following a path that would make money. But it wasn't because I needed it—it was because it gave me an excuse to disengage with people and experiences that were risky. This journey was an attempt to flip that paradigm.

But Rick and Darby—and Sean and Kendra—were in a constant state of risk, forced at every turn to rely on each other and anyone else who came along. They had the risk by default.

"Kendra, can you read?"

She looked at her mom, who nodded slightly. Kendra looked back at me and nodded, too.

"Great, you want to help me look at this map?"

"Okay." She stepped beside me while I unfolded the yellowed and faded map.

"So I was dropped here, you see? And now we're . . . here. And I think the hotel is here. But help me look for a free clinic, okay? It might be marked with a red or green cross . . ."

"There's one!" She pointed at the general hospital on the north side of town.

"Yes, right. That's good. Now let's look for one closer to where we are—right here."

Her brother walked between us and she scooted a bit to let him in, his nose peeking over the edge of the map.

"What's that?" he asked, pointing to a random highway, marked with red and blue lines.

"That, Sean, is an interstate."

"An *interest* state?"

I smiled, and Kendra leaned forward.

"How about that?" she asked, lightly touching her finger to the middle of the map. I bent forward to see.

"Let's stop beneath this streetlight." I held the map up closer, and saw it: a clinic not two blocks from where we were.

"Rick, I think we're in luck, my friend."

The grimace on his face eased a bit, and Darby touched his left arm lightly.

This family had an obvious closeness and bond for each other; they were committed and were genuinely close. They seemed happy. There was a glow emanating from all of them. A glow that spoke volumes for their state of mind. It reminded me of the time I wandered through the slums of Mumbai, India. The level of poverty was all pervasive yet the camaraderie and love that emanated from the people was astonishing. They genuinely seemed content with life. I know this sounds difficult to fathom, but they had the same glow that this American family possessed. An American family that was most certainly not living the American dream, yet one that on the face of it, seemed content. They possessed an inner glow that certainly eluded me. I would go so far as say that they possessed the same thing that the slum children in Mumbai possessed. A fire inside that transcended their situation. They were *happy* and provided me an exquisite example of how the intricacies of human connection can lift people from external situations that may seem hopeless.

We reached the corner of our separation, and I reached out my hand to Darby.

"Best of luck, you guys. A pleasure walking with you. Kendra, Sean—you're the best map readers I've ever met. Rick, you should be proud."

"I am, I am."

"Take care of yourself."

"And you, Leon. Be careful out there."

The family I had stumbled across on the outskirts of downtown Indianapolis inadvertently sparked a firestorm of emotional reflection. What an opportunity I was being faced with. Traveling around America living on the kindness of strangers meeting inspirational people along the path was reenergizing my world. I said my heartfelt goodbyes to my new friends and wished the father good luck in his attempts to get medical help. As I continued on my way to the hotel, with my head filled with the emotional and psychological debris of this encounter, I forgot about the policeman's warning.

I was soon to be reminded.

My time with the kids and family had buoyed me, but now alone, each step closer to the heart of downtown Indianapolis created further unease. I tried to stay good-natured (and alive) giving a short smile and shorter greeting to each ragged person I passed.

"What you doing, boy?" came a gruff voice from a side alley.

I ignored it, but it seemed the man was adamant about becoming my *friend.* He repeated the question, this time with a little more menace.

"'What you doing, boy,' I said! You deaf!"

I weighed my options and concluded that ignoring this chap was a mistake. Despite having felt fear and trepidation a number of times on my trip, this was the first time I felt truly threatened; that I might actually suffer physical harm. This moment was different. I sensed a growing belligerence. I slowed down and faced him.

My goal was to exit the imminent encounter unscathed. I wasn't sure whether he was simply a drunk carrying a bottle or carrying something more sinister.

"Hey man, I am just on my way to a hotel, can I help you?"

"You got any money, boy?"

Here goes, I was thinking to myself.

"Actually I am from London and I am not carrying cash with me today, sorry." Englishmen apologize for everything. Here I was apologizing to a man who seemed intent on making my life miserable at best. He didn't like my response. Instead of taking out a gun and spraying me with bullets he continued belligerently, "How can you not have *no* money, boy!"

Explaining that was not going to be an easy one. I doubted he was going to believe I was traveling around America relying on the kindness of strangers. I made a judgment call that the situation wasn't ripe for this discussion. I changed the subject.

"Listen man, I am really tired. I am going to go to my hotel now." I started to move out of his path.

"He put his hand back into his pocket. "That would be a wrong move." I was rooted to the spot. Fear coursing through my body, I realized that making a move to leave would bring with it the potential of unwanted consequences. I backed away slowly.

"Okay, I'll stay. What do you want from me," I stammered.

"Why does everyone think I want something from them?"

Well, you're not allowing me to leave and you're intimating that you have a gun. So you obviously want something, I said to myself. But outwardly, I remained silent, still rooted to the spot.

"Do you want to buy a rock?"

Great, this guy was trying to sell drugs to someone who was practically penniless. The situation would have been humorous if it wasn't so scary.

I didn't want to antagonize the guy by reminding him that I didn't actually have any money, so instead I politely declined.

"Man, the problem is that people don't have their perspective on life in the right place!" The guy was getting philosophical. I had stumbled on the only philosophical drug dealer in America. Fitting, I suppose, after the only wrestling priest in America. I suppose there might be others of both, but have you heard of any?

He continued to ramble incoherently about people not having the right perspective—was buying drugs the "right perspective" I wondered—and as I listened, I cautiously attempted various ways out of the situation. Whenever I tried casually to wander toward the alley entrance, he blocked my path. Whenever he paused, and I tried to slip away, he'd start back up again. My nerves were fraying at the edges. During the half hour he literally held me hostage, I noticed that as long as I listened quietly and stayed rooted to the spot, he mellowed. When I tried to respond or escape, his aggression resurfaced. I had no choice but to sit and listen. This gave me ample time to think.

I realized the moment had a lesson in it: I was far removed from my comfort zone, as far as I'd ever ventured—in a dank alley that smelled of urine with a drug dealer in downtown Indianapolis. If I could muster the inner strength to live and thrive in this moment, I could do this in my everyday world. There was a reason for everything I had experienced so far. And those experiences, both good and bad, could shape my future. Insight comes at the oddest of times, and at this moment my captor was giving me a chance to practice for the rest of my life. After this, nothing would be too weird to handle, no social engagement too awkward to push through.

"And another thing! The economy! The economy has us all in the hole. We got a business, they take it away—"

He raised his voice, and I realized a night watchman across the street had taken notice of the scene. I tried getting his attention by waving subtly, and jerking my head toward the dealer. My sign language didn't seem to be working and the last thing I wanted was for my drug dealing friend to see me hailing for help. Eventually the doorman seemed to understand the potential seriousness of the situation. I saw him walk to his desk and pick up the phone; I prayed it was to dial the police and not one of his friends to tell them that he was about to witness a murder. Less than five minutes later, I could hear sirens, and soon lights were flashing between the buildings as two police cars appeared. I half-expected to see the cop from the freeway again, and prepared myself for the inevitable lecture I was sure to receive.

A policeman asked me what was going on, and since I was not about to tell them that this guy was trying to sell me drugs while he was standing within ear shot, I kept it simple: I told them that this gentleman was not letting me leave, I felt unsafe, and all I wanted was to be able to get to the hotel unscathed. Even this appeared not to be the right answer from his point of view—maybe he thought we were having a good time?—and he shot me a threatening look just as the cops were encouraging me to go on my way, with clear directions for how to get to hotel. I hoped that the police didn't let this guy go before I had found my way there.

I kept looking over my shoulder to make sure the guy was not following me. The police were not arresting him, but they were having stern words. If ever I'd been anxious to see the friendly face of Mrs. Adams, it was now. I was terribly late for our appointment, and managed to get myself lost once more on the way to the hotel, but somehow I turned a corner and there they were—the welcoming lights of the Marriot glowing in the distance. A few blocks more and I reached my nirvana, a welcoming sight if ever I'd seen one. In the marble lobby sat Mrs. Adams, waiting diligently on the sofa. She stood up immediately, smiled warmly, and came over to give me a welcome hug.

I needed that hug.

"Leon! It's great that you're here. Did you have a hard time getting here?"

I smiled. "You could say that," I answered, but refrained from detailing the entire journey from the freeway. "This hotel is nice—too nice. I don't want you spending too much on me."

"Oh, nonsense. You were a wonderful traveling companion on the train, and we're honored to be a part of your journey. Here, I brought you some snacks . . ." She handed me a plastic bag stuffed with all kinds of goodies: peanut butter and jelly sandwiches, cookies, candy bars, cokes, chocolates, and more.

On the day I learn I'm skidding toward diabetes, a woman I hardly know gives me a bag full of thousands of calories of sugary sweets. Nice one, Universe. Very funny.

"Oh, thank you! I don't know what to say!" I really didn't. How about, "Thanks! I can't wait to go into a diabetic coma!" This may have been a little dramatic and also it was unnecessary to share my doctor's report from the morning. (Was it only just that morning? It seemed so long ago, Ashley and the truck stop and the call from my mother. It's amazing how the days expand on such a journey.)

"You look exhausted, young man. Get some rest." She touched my arm. "And if you need anything else, well, you have my number." She kissed me on the cheek and said farewell, handing me the room key. I looked down at it—Room 324—inside the small little booklet they give you at posh hotels. The receipt was in there as well: Mrs. Adams had purchased a hotel room for $112.

How could she have spent so much on a complete stranger? Astonishing really. Random acts of kindness never really make sense. And that's their charm—they exist outside of reason and rationale. My connections were always so fleeting. That this one with Mrs. Adams had come full circle was a particular blessing.

I found my way up to the room and could not have been

happier to fall on the bed. My stomach growled and I stared at the clock: 11 p.m. I was starving. It was time to turn on the charm again.

I crawled off the bed, took a quick shower, put on some lotion to smell charming and wandered downstairs to the restaurant, which was a few minutes from closing. After the moments spent in a hostage situation with a drug dealer, and having considered how dramatic that situation was in comparison with any other moment I might have felt afraid, I walked confidently up to the server. Twenty minutes later, I had wrangled my way to a roast chicken dinner. I paid with the few remaining dollars I had left. By midnight I was in bed with a full belly, grateful and satisfied.

Whilst dozing off I reflected on the simple fact that I no longer felt afraid. Rather than feeling traumatized, I felt free. As free as Chris's paroled prisoners, as free as Mrs. Adams, as free as Ashley, as free as I might ever be.

That I'd never felt this way before was due to a habit of fear. My escapades with the drug dealer had put me face-to-face with a primal fear, yet the type of fear that kept me stuck for so many years seemed of greater depth and ferocity. It was a fear that clouded my judgment. Its presence seemed to defy the everyday situations I found myself in yet its hold over me was complete. My inability to follow my true dreams being a major way that fear infiltrated my life.

I feared change.

I feared rejection.

I feared failure.

It was fear that led me to go to business school instead of accepting a soccer scholarship that my father felt fostered a "pipe dream." It was fear that lead me to my job, to break off my relationships, to live alone. Such capitulation to fear ruled my life for decades and came close to destroying me. My encounter with the illiterate American family showed me that no matter what we are faced with we *can* adapt. As a species we are innately resourceful and have the capacity to reshape our own destinies. The type of fear I experienced with the drug dealer was visceral, yet the fear I allowed to rule my life had been harder to identify and therefore even more destabilizing. I needed to reprogram myself and work from current reality, not that of a frightened child.

I was an adult.

Sounds simple, but it's sometimes the simple things that elude us.

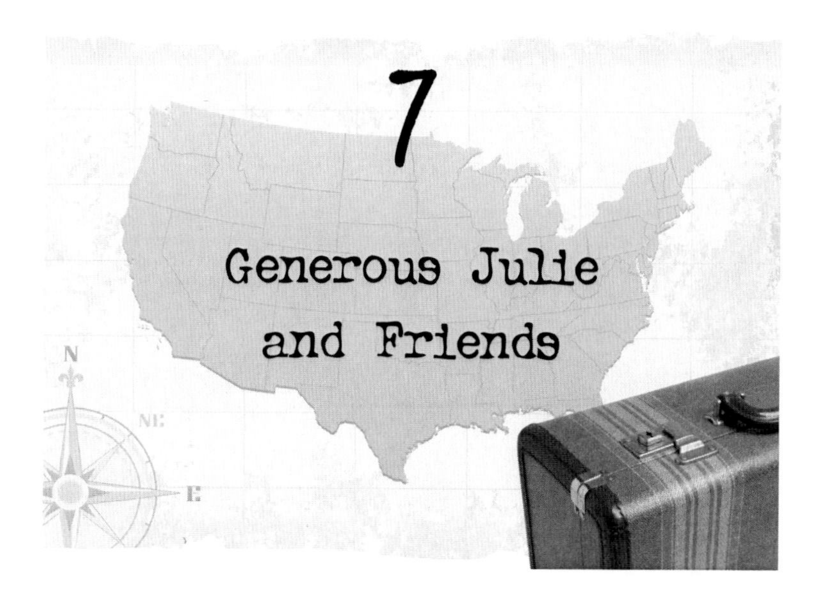

7
Generous Julie and Friends

What this world needs is a new kind of army—
the army of the kind.

—Cleveland Amory

The next morning I woke up and immediately forsook any notion of common sense, gulping down two cookies and three cupcakes from the stash Mrs. Adams had so graciously purchased for me. It definitely tasted good, but within an hour, I felt far from good, in fact a little bit like hell. I then spent another two hours sleeping off the headache I'd given myself. Lesson learned.

I checked out late morning and sat myself on the bench outside the hotel contemplating my next move. A red-haired woman who appeared to be in her mid-thirties was sitting in a car, getting ready to unload her suitcases. I started up a conversation that would lead to a moment of generosity that to this day has baffled and amazed me in equal doses.

"Are you going to Chicago?" I felt that Chicago was the nearest big city so why not try and get there today.

"She is," said another lady who popped out of the car. "But not till tomorrow."

"Oh, too bad. Okay, thanks." I said, a bit downhearted. My head still hurting a bit.

"Do you need to go now?" responded the friend.

"Yeah, I'm trying to get to Chicago today," I said.

"Where you from?" the redhead inquired.

"London," I said, and took the liberty of going on to explain the trip and the goals I had set for myself.

"Surf the country on a wave of generosity . . ." said the redhead.

"Exactly!" I replied. "That's a beautiful way to put it."

I could feel the fuse had been lit within them, as had happened before. Telling the story as many times as I had, the reaction often seemed a desire to be part of it, to stand up and say "Look at me! I'm kind! I'm kind!"

I took it as far as I could, and ran for the goalpost. "Can I have your car?"

"My car?" she asked, a glint in her eye.

"Yeah, you know, to find my way to Chicago." I feigned seriousness.

Unbelievably, I could see she was actually contemplating it. This lady who had never met me before was thinking about giving me her car. I could not accept this so I put an end to it.

"No, no! I was only kidding. I wouldn't expect you to give me your car! Sorry—bad joke. I can't believe you were thinking about it!"

But she wasn't deterred. Without missing a beat, she uttered some magical words. "If you want, you can stay at our place tonight in Chicago. If you can figure out a way to get there."

"Tonight?" her friend said, a little surprised.

It turned out that my new red-headed friend and her one year old son, Elliot, were in town for a relative's wedding and they would be returning to their home in Chicago the following day after the festivities ended.

I was shocked. "Are you offering me to stay in your house when you're not there?" I said bewildered.

"Yeah, I guess I am."

What the fuck! I was literally lost for words and barely managed to mumble, "I mean the whole point of this is the generosity . . . and by your saying this to me, I'm in shock—in good shock—but honestly . . ."

". . . don't even know how to deal with it?" her friend responded.

"Basically."

"The question remains, though: how do you get there?"

This was actually going to happen.

"Oh, trust me. If you're giving me your place, I'll make it to Chicago." I had no idea how. But I had to take advantage of this.

"Great. So let me give you directions."

It was all surreal. Here I was getting instructions from a woman I didn't even know, to get to a city I'd never been to, to find a street I'd never heard of, and use her keys to enter her empty house. Dangling the keys in front of me she said, "Here you go; now, we're assuming you're going to find your way there, so we're guessing we can get these back tomorrow? Just drop them in the flower pot next to the door when you leave."

"Just . . . drop them in the flower pot?" I stared at the keys like they were my absent cell phone. This was too much.

"Yeah. Geraniums. You'll see it."

"Okay, you got it." I pocketed the keys and told myself to stop grinning like an idiot. Was I missing something?

"Wait!" I said, as the two women were walking toward the lobby. "I, uh, I don't know your name!"

She smiled widely. "I'm Julie."

"Julie, I will take good care of your house and gift your keys to the geraniums and tell the world of your generosity for many years to come."

She just laughed and walked through the automatic doors. I stood in the parking lot, my headache gone, and my mind reeling. I mean, who does this?

A cabbie had just dropped a woman at the door, and was parked next to the hotel reading a paper. I noticed he had been watching this entire episode unfold, so figured that he would want to show his kind spirit as well.

I was right.

He was sitting there, probably waiting for a fare. Going up to his window, I asked, "Will you drive me to Chicago?"

"Sure, hop in!" He was smiling. I knew he was joking, but I would go as far as he'd take me.

"Can you believe this?" I asked.

"That's one nice lady you hit up. I gotta try your schtick sometime."

"Tell me about it."

"Next time I pick up a customer, I think I'm gonna ask him, 'Hey, I usually charge fifty cents a mile, but instead, why don't you give me your house. Apparently people are giving them away pretty easily.'"

"I know! I almost thought she was playing me or something."

"But you got the keys in your pocket."

"Yes, I do." I still couldn't believe it. "So, I have a house. Can I have a ride?"

"You betcha. Can't let myself be outdone by a woman from Chicago."

"So, where to? How far can I beg a ride?"

"I can drive you to the truck stop down the road . . ."

"Couldn't ask for more!"

The guy was a blast. My new friend told me how he once persuaded a stranger to propose to his girlfriend as a joke. Another time he smashed someone's face in, when the man made the unfortunate decision of trying to rob him. ("You messed with the wrong man!" were the last words the robber heard before falling into a state of unconsciousness.) Another time he'd driven the German ambassador to a private meeting with investors. Said he smelled funny. This journey was fast becoming an episode from HBO's *Taxicab Confessions,* but it was the driver who was doing all the confessing.

"Most of the time they ask me, do you have a camera in your cab, I say no, so then they start talking, you know, *yap yap yap yap yap.* They're like 'I'm not going to see him again so what the heck. I'll tell him my entire life story.' So people tell you all their life story, man, for like a twenty minute drive. They tell you about their marriage, their wife and kids, and all of that."

"You ever had a woman try and hook up with you?" I inquired playfully.

"Yeah, all the time!" he said with a big smile. "I mean, look at me, Leon. I'm a gorgeous, irresistible man." He laughed heartily. "But I'm married, you can't do it, you know what I'm saying?"

Ten minutes later, he pulled into a gas station and turned to wave me out of his cab.

"Trucks come here, too. You can hitch a ride with one of the drivers."

"Abe, you are as honest and good as your name suggests. I thank you, sir."

"Leon, you are as odd and amiable as your name suggests. Good luck!"

"Hey, what's up? Where you headed?"

Abe hadn't been gone half a minute before a couple pulled up in an old Honda Civic and hollered their hello.

"Oh, hi! I'm going to Chicago."

"Cool! We're going to a monster truck rally!" said the girl, who looked twenty, at most.

"In Chicago?"

"No! In North Indianapolis! It's gonna be awesome!"

"Are you a trucker?"

"Huh?"

"You know, a monster trucker?"

They looked at each other and laughed. "No, man! We're just going to watch."

"Okay, then. I'm off to find a ride. Good to meet you."

The girl stopped her friend and called out again, "We can take you. Maybe."

I spun around. This was too easy.

"Really? But you're going—"

"Yeah, to the rally . . . but after that. You know, when it's done."

"Oh, absolutely. I'll just wait outside of the monster truck place and come with you guys . . ."

But I saw hesitancy. "Oh," said the guy, "well, we're kind of going on a date though."

"Oh, you're going on a date! Oh, my God! I'd ruin your date!"

"Here," said Emily, reaching for a pen in the glove compartment. "Take our cell number and call us in a few hours if you don't have a ride, okay?"

"Sounds good . . ." And they were off. A prospect, but nothing guaranteed. I had to keep looking.

I started to approach another car when I overheard a group of bikers talking about me several yards away.

". . . trying to con people!" I heard one of them say.

". . . 'shamed of himself. He certainly doesn't seem like he needs the money."

" . . . leech." One of the women responded.

". . . tell the authorities . . . guy's bad news."

I couldn't hear everything, but heard enough to be consumed with shame. Obviously I was not taking people's money, as I couldn't accept money. I knew this, they didn't. They were making assumptions. My first reaction was to leave it alone and not waste time reacting, but there was something inside me that forced a reaction. I didn't want to leave this alone. I wanted to respond and put the record straight. I wanted them to realize what it was that I was actually doing. Look, if after I told them they still felt I was a leech then so be it.

But they were a large group—in number (about fifteen) and size (intimidating). They wore leather and straddled big road bikes. Basically the kind you see in the movies. Not the type of people you want to mess with. Certainly not the type of people *I* wanted to mess with.

But I thought of the drug dealer and being a hostage in an alley. Fear was no longer in control. I mustered the courage to approach them.

"Excuse me, I couldn't help but overhear your comments," I said with as much kind confidence as I could. "And I wanted to set the record straight." And so I did, informing them of the real reasons for the trip, explaining how I was unable to accept money and that I was doing this as a way to find out more about life and those around me. I apologized for barging in on the conversation, but told them it was necessary to put the record straight.

I'd barely finished when one of the men with the group who hadn't heard my opening explanation barged past me.

"Is this man causing a scene?"

Fortunately his friends reassured him that things were good and I was not a threat. I hate to think what would have happened had they said I *was* a threat. The mood quickly lightened as they digested what I was telling them and seemed genuinely happy to talk.

"That's cool. We just thought that you were a con man going up to people and asking them for money," one of the smaller guys said.

"Your story is actually pretty inspiring. It's wonderful to see how so many people have helped you along the way. It inspires me to believe that things are not all that bad in this world of ours."

"You know what mate? That is so true. That's one of the major things I have taken from the trip. A sense of renewal, a sense of acceptance that the world is not as I once saw it.

There is great potential in each and every one of us to love and be gracious. I never realized this until I embarked on this odyssey. I was always looking at life from the dark side, yet there is a light that so many of us fail to see."

It was true.

"We would find a way to help you, but unfortunately we are on our way to New York City! If you want to go back east then hop on!"

I thanked them for their offer and felt a surge of pride rise through my soul. I had faced them, faced my fear, and won them over.

It was a small victory that came before a series of defeats.

I asked twelve people over the next hour for a ride toward Chicago. Not one of them replied positively. Despite the recent positive experiences, I was starting to worry. To add to my woes, a female gas station attendant approached and started speaking loudly even before she reached me.

"Please stop loitering in the station; I am going to have to ask you to leave the premises."

"Oh, I am not loitering, I'm . . ."

She interrupted, "Sir, I am responsible for the station and I have had numerous complaints from people that you are harassing them and soliciting them for favors."

"Favors? No, no. I am just trying to get a ride, surely this is not a crime," I pleaded.

"I will repeat: people have claimed that you are trying to solicit them for favors and this is unacceptable. This is private property and I will not ask you again. If you do not leave I will call the police." My time in Indianapolis had already been blighted by two unfortunate encounters with the law and I was highly motivated to avoid a third. Given no choice, I agreed to leave. I felt shame. I didn't want people to feel threatened, yet it seemed I had definitely outstayed my welcome. The fact that people had complained was not ideal. It made me question myself. Was I a mooch? Was I overstepping other people's boundaries?

I didn't really have much time to ponder. I needed to get to Chicago, and—more urgently—I needed to get off the premises. The lady was monitoring me from inside the station and gestured to the phone as if to say, "I am going to call the police."

Hoisting my rucksack to my shoulders, I started walking across the plaza toward the highway. Another station sat nearby, and I walked briskly toward it, hoping my friend at the other station hadn't sent out the alert to all the others. When I arrived, there was a ginger-haired chap pumping gas. I didn't want the same thing to happen as it had in the previous station, so I was hoping that this was going to work itself out quickly and quietly.

"You busy? Can you give me a ride out of this gas station?"

"Where you headed, son?"

He was in his early fifties, but had the same youthful energy as a college frat boy; filled to the brim with life.

"Chicago."

"Chicago's not far. But I can't do that. What's in Chicago anyway?"

And so the story came spilling out, culminating in the free house that had been offered to me by a stranger in a parking lot.

"Well, how about that. You know . . . ." He was thinking, pulled out his cell phone and checked the time. "I have an idea."

Enthralled by my accent and the purpose of my journey, he invited me over to his home for a true midwestern barbecue.

"Whoa, that'd be great, but . . . are you sure it's okay with the family?" I asked. I didn't want any unpleasant surprises.

"Let me give Mama a call, put some more chicken on the grill, this is bad to the bone . . . hey, look at them big boys." This last statement was a side note when a rather attractive lady walked by. He called his wife, and I listened: "You ready for this wild story? I'm bringing a young chap home from London to come eat your chicken." It seemed he had to assuage her fears that I was not going to stay the night as well. "No, he's going to Chicago tonight."

"Okay! To the house."

"So, do you normally pick up Englishmen in gas stations?" I enquired.

"Good question Leon!" he laughed. "Can't say I've ever met an Englishman at a gas station. Maybe this'll be the start of a tradition. Every time I meet an English guy, he's coming over for a barbecue!"

"I'm sure my countrymen would like that!"

"C'mon," Joe said excitedly. "Ma's getting everything ready."

Fifteen minutes later, we pulled into the stony drive of a simple one-story home on the outskirts of Indianapolis.

"Okay, we're here! Let's go party! Wanna drink some beer?"

Things were looking up. Not for long.

An angry lady stormed out the front door, and Joe stopped smiling. So did I. It seemed that Joe had not properly explained my presence to her. She went on a tirade at poor old Joe for bringing home a complete stranger. It seemed that my stay with them was going to be an extraordinarily brief one. I felt so uncomfortable that I insisted on walking back to the station, and apologized profusely for the intrusion.

She wasn't listening. She continued going off on her husband, whose earlier communication skills seemed to have deserted him.

Things started to calm down when I took his wife—whose name, I learned, was Carole—aside and explained my situation. She stood with me outside on the porch, as I explained that Joe must have felt sorry for me and just wanted to do a good deed. The fact that I was helped by him had made my day. His ability to show kindness and grace had lifted my spirits. I could see Carole's face soften as I reassured her that I understood my visit was inconvenient, and I'd just go on back to the station and get a ride to continue my journey. The last thing I wanted was to be a burden.

My intervention seemed to change her mind. I was not going to have to start out again, just yet. Carole reassured me that I was in fact welcome; it was just that her husband had not really explained on the phone what was going on.

"That man can't keep anything straight. But come on, Leon. Help me get this chicken ready."

The party was now officially on.

Within half an hour the potent smell of grilled chicken was drifting from the backyard, and the strangest thing happened: neighbors started showing up. First a couple from next door walked into the yard—they had a big pot of vegetables with them. Then a family from down the road poked their head over the fence and Joe waved them over, a couple of six packs in their hands. Soon Carole was warming up green beans and boiling corn. It was going to be a feast for the neighborhood, and I'd never seen anything like it. When we were all ready to sit down for the meal there were about fifteen people with all the new arrivals. Joe made a toast and the crowd raised their beers:

"To Carole, who can multiply food into a feast faster than Jesus!"

"To Carole!" echoed the group.

I sat back with a Diet Coke and chatted with the neighbors. It was a truly wonderful experience to be sitting with strangers enjoying their company. We talked about everything from politics to the state of the latest boy band crazes. That is the magical thing when you actually just sit down with people, even strangers: you talk.

In London, as in many larger cities, a sense of community has all but been extinguished. To experience the level of hospitality and the welcoming spirit of total strangers you have to leave the urban density and anonymity and find smaller communities. Here was one. And it definitely gave me a sense of belonging. They didn't have to embrace me; no obligation brought me here. Yet they chose to open their arms to a stranger and help me along on my path. I was honored that after a slightly rocky start they welcomed me into their world.

The festivities with Joe, Carole, and the gang made me lose track of time and the necessity I faced: finding my way to Chicago. I looked at my watch, realized it was nearly 9 p.m., and reached out to my last hope: Emily and her monster-truck loving friend. The rest of my night hung in the balance.

I called my last great hope for a ride, and was pleasantly shocked when she said she and her friend would be able to drive me to Chicago. They were on their way, and had stories of the truck rally to keep me entertained along the drive.

Joe had passed out on the sofa and Carole insisted that I wake him up to say my good-byes. I felt sadness leaving their home; they had taken me in and it had been such a warm experience, like a Christmas dinner where the whole family is present and the feelings of contentment and satisfaction are rampant. Carole and Joe epitomized the type of family connection I yearned for. I said good-bye with a bit of sadness, and Joe gave me a sleepy, inebriated hug as Emily and monster-truck man pulled into the driveway to pick me up.

I laughed all the way to Chicago. The caffeine from the Diet Coke, the tasty chicken, and the good conversation had put me in fantastic spirits, and Emily and Jay (he only told me his name right before they dropped me off) had a youthful energy that matched my mood. The world was beautiful, the night was clear, we were all in perfect spirits, and life was as it should be.

We stopped once for gas, and I chipped in my daily allowance. I got to thinking that Jay had originally not wanted to give me a lift to Chicago as he was taking Emily on their first date. Well, what a date this had turned out to be. I couldn't help thinking how this date was one that they would never forget.

The hours, like the miles, flew by, and I got out the address Julie had written down for me and helped Jay navigate through the streets of Chicago by calling out street names and landmarks. Soon Julie's apartment building beckoned and they dropped me off right outside her door. I bade farewell to the young lovers and turned to Julie's door.

The next thirty minutes were a slight blur.

In my deep shock that she'd given me her *home*, I had not listened to the exact instructions Julie gave me about the keys to be used or even her door number. This was going to cause a problem. There must have been thirty keys on her key ring. I began trying them one at a time.

After twenty-one keys, I finally opened the front door.

When I entered the building, I was faced with three more doors, and I had no idea which one was Julie's. I tried desperately to remember, but it was past midnight and my weary mind wouldn't recall the morning's instructions. I looked at door one, door two, and door three, and prayed that my choice didn't reveal danger, but much needed sleep.

I was on key fifteen for door number one, when I heard rustling inside and quickly backed away. Then I remembered: Julie had told me to be very quiet because there was a family of six living in the building and they would no doubt be confused if they saw me.

My mind started doing what it does best: freaking me out. I thought about how if I was trying to enter the wrong door I could quite feasibly be shot. I recalled that in America you are legally allowed to shoot someone who is breaking in to your home. If this was not Julie's door, I was trying to break into someone else's house. And it was dead of night. Statistically there was a 66 percent chance that this was in fact the wrong door. I imagined a young mother huddled in bed with her four children and her irate husband getting his pump action shotgun ready for discharge! I backed off door number one.

I then gave up on door number two after ten minutes and too much fear. This left one last door. I pulled out a random key stuck it in the lock, and turned. Unbelievable! It opened on my first try (which was really like my fortieth overall). As I found my way into Julie's apartment I heard a commotion next door and I was now rightfully worried that the family of six had called the police who would soon be barging down Julie's door thinking I was an intruder. I could just see how I was going to try and explain that one away. Pushing through the entrance; I fervently hoped the guy next door had not called the police. I shut the door firmly behind me. There was no way I was going outside again. The place was neat and clean, almost as if waiting for a guest. I found the bathroom, washed up and got ready for bed. It had been a long and eventful day.

I needed sleep. Badly.

I made up a bed on the couch and was getting ready to turn off the light when there was a loud knock at the door.

Who the hell was that?

The police? It had to be. I couldn't apportion any blame to the guy next door if he had actually called the cops but if it was the police I was in big shit. How was I going to explain my situation to them? I had no proof that Julie had actually given me the keys. The neighbors would have no idea who I was. I fervently hoped it was not the police, although if it was a shotgun wielding neighbor I would have definitely preferred it be the police. I was in a pickle and completely alone. I was probably fucked.

"Yes?" I said, opening the front door a couple of inches.

A pretty young woman's face peered through the door. "Hi," she grinned. "I'm Mary, Julie's next-door neighbor. Julie called and told me what was going on."

Relief washed over me. "Hi, I'm Leon. Your neighbor is the nicest person in America."

"My neighbor is classic, and a bit spontaneous. But so am I. Must be a neighborhood thing."

"Right. Friendly place."

"So . . . can I come in for a chat?"

Grateful that it was not the police or the shotgun wielding neighbor, I agreed.

She sat on the couch, and we talked for about an hour, about my life, about hers. She was married, though not happily it seemed, and she seemed lonely.

"So, can I show you the neighborhood? Great bar just around the corner. Should be a nice crowd right now."

"Uh . . . it's nearly three in the morning."

"Yeah, but that's when it gets interesting!"

I was in no state to go partying, and all I wanted was to get into my makeshift bed. Though I wanted to latch onto any opportunity to connect, this open door should probably stay closed. I declined her offer. Though she was persistent, I eventually managed to coax her out of the apartment and soon fell into a deep sleep.

The next morning I overslept, waking up a little after nine. Around ten, I was ready to leave when there was another knock at the door. Maybe this time it was the police. Thankfully it was Julie and Elliot, who had come home early. Seeing them again reminded me that the entire scenario I found myself in was unprecedented, and likely unrepeatable; a young woman with nothing to gain and much to lose offers me a space in her life and her home.

I happily spent the majority of the morning with them. I actually became a supervised babysitter for a while and enjoyed my time with the little one. As if Julie had not done enough for me she offered to take me to the train station and buy me a ticket to continue on my journey west. Generous Julie was certainly staying true to her new nickname.

After spending a little more time playing with Elliot, we got in the car and moved onto the station. Julie kept her word and bought me a ticket for Galesburg, Illinois, slightly west of Chicago. I hugged both Julie and Elliott farewell, leaving behind yet another piece of my heart.

8
The Good People of Galesburg

A man travels the world over in search
of what he needs and returns home to find it.

—*George Moore*

The train ride to Galesburg was uneventful. The few passengers slept or read, leaving me to my own devices. Illinois is beautiful place. The land is flat, but the trees and rivers seem to work together to make the most of an unimaginative topography. It was a peaceful journey, and as I'd felt in Chicago, there was so much to be gained by having no monetary obligations. The sense of freedom had settled on me.

Upon reaching Galesburg, I asked a railway employee where the mayor's office was. I had a plan. While on the train I realized that I'd had no interaction with the famous

American political system. The great democratic government that has inspired the world was still unknown to me (save my uncomfortable interactions with the police). So I was off to ask the mayor of this leafy midwestern town if he would put me up for the night. It sounded like a good idea at the time. It turned out to be not such a good idea.

I stopped at what I thought was the mayor's office.

"G'day, friend! Can I speak with the mayor?" I asked.

"The mayor? The mayor doesn't have an office at police headquarters."

Jesus. The police. Again.

"Simple mistake. How about I speak with the chief of police then?" I asked.

"What business do you have with the chief?" the policeman behind the counter snarled. Then he noticed the microphone on my lapel.

"Is that a microphone?" he asked sharply. "Are you recording this conversation?"

"No, of course not!"

"Then why do you have a microphone on?"

"Oh, it's not on." Actually, it was on. I don't know why I said it wasn't. But it was too late. I then tried charming him by explaining my journey and that I was on a mission to gauge the kindness of strangers. He was completely uninterested and kept on about the fact that I was taping him.

"Listen, boy, if you are taping this conversation we will have a problem!"

What is it about American law enforcement personnel and the propensity to use the word *boy*? With a quick apology, I left the station, hoping he wouldn't follow. He didn't. Just as I walked out of the police building, I was stopped by two black guys and a girl. One of them had just been released from the station and had overheard what happened with the policeman.

"Where you from, man?" the taller guy asked.

"London, but I am on my way to the Hollywood sign."

"I heard what was going on with the cop. You can't mess with these dudes! They don't got no soul!"

"Yeah, he didn't seem too pleased with me, but what the hell . . ."

The guy wanted to make up for my unpleasant experience with the policeman and offered to buy me some food—an offer I never refused. In minutes I was presented with a cheeseburger and fries, courtesy of Dre and a buddy of his who had just arrived at the deli we had entered. I couldn't actually eat the cheeseburger and fries due to my illness but I dared not divulge this information. I held onto it tightly and hoped they would not force me to chomp it down.

Over the next fifteen minutes or so, cars—lots of them—filled to the brim with Dre's friends, pulled up outside the deli. Soon the place was swarming with people.

One moment I was having a pleasant chat with two guys and a girl and then it seemed as though the entire neighborhood descended up on us. And they all had questions:

"You from London? Man, that's a long way off. I been to New York, tho."

"You seen V for Vendetta? Love it when they blow up that big clock."

"What kinda music they listen to in London?

"So you basically . . . how are you gonna get somewhere when you've got no money?"

And so I told my story. The story of Cinnamon and

generous Julie and Chris and the Adams' and the wrestling preacher and the frat boys in Virginia, and so many more.

"So where you staying tonight?" Dre asked.

"Don't know. But I'll find a place. Any ideas?"

"I got an idea," said a short fellow next to Dre. He spun his hat around and sat down next to me. "You rap for your room."

"Excuse me?"

"Rap. You can rap, right? So you rap and if you any good, we'll give you a place to stay."

I thought about it. This could work. I'd never rapped before, but how hard could it be? Find words that rhyme, put them in a few sentences, wave your hands. I could do this.

"I accept!"

A cheer went up.

Then things got interesting.

"I'll start, then throw to you. You ready?" Dre's friend, Mario, asked. I didn't have time to say no.

"Leon, this bloke is a jolly good fellow,
chilling with a bunch of black dudes while his skin
be yellow.
It don't mean nothing, homey.
Leon got no homey . . .

Then he pointed to me.

"Uhh . . . I'm rapping and rhyming but I don't know
what I'm saying,
While my homey at the grill is busy with fillet . . . ing.

A cheer! So I continued.

> "He's making burgers and fries and they're very very tasty.
> Look at me, I rhymed even though my skin is pasty!

A cheer again! I was making it. Mario took over.

> You're white but missed your flight,
> I'm black just out of state pack.
> You don't like me, then stay outa my way,
> This little dude's living on five dollars a day . . .

He threw it back to me, and I was feeling good. Too good. My sense of glory was about to come crashing down.

> That's right I'm living on five dollars a day.

Then, I blanked. Nothing. What rhymes with day? Come on, Leon! Think!

> And I like hay, cause it doesn't cost much . . .

I was lost. *Hay?* What the hell? Now what rhymes with much? Damn it!

Mario saved me:

> It do cost much, but you got to roll it up.

I smiled and the crowd laughed. He continued:

> You roll it up and smoke it and you're happy with your life.

He pointed to me.

"Uhh . . . ." The crowd was waiting. "I, uhh . . ." I was embarrassed and nothing was going to come to me. He took it back.

> Today, You smoke it and you smoke it and you don't
> shook twice.

A whoop from the deli crowd, as he continued.

> You only shook twice if you smoke it the wrong way.
> If you smoke it the wrong way, your ass gonna get
> sprayed.

He pointed to me as the crowd started swaying to his beat. I continued as best I could—pathetically:

> And if you get sprayed, then you might as well live in
> a field of hay.

Total silence.

The dancing stopped. Everyone stared at me and then stared at each other. *Hay, Leon? Hay?*

Then piercing the silence, the sound of sirens.

The crowd cleared as quickly as they'd come. Within thirty seconds, the deli was empty. I was sitting alone with my untouched burger, wondering what on earth had just happened.

"Was I that bad?" I asked the man at the register.

"You weren't good."

Well, that was true. My rapping had run them off? That, and the promise of cops. One minute I was the center of attention in this strange world of American gangster rap, the next I was completely alone as they all fired up their engines and disappeared. My attempt to garner a free room had ended in total humiliation. I grabbed my backpack and walked out, the cheeseburger and fries in hand. Two steps out the door, I realized I was still holding them, and when I was out of eyeshot of its maker, I tossed them in the bushes.

The town center loomed ahead, but didn't look promising. It was now evening, and I wondered how I would find a person to help me out. There were few people walking the streets, and for someone who relies on connecting with people to sustain himself this was a bad sign. Fate, however, had something different in store for me on this brisk evening. The streets were completely empty, so I figured crossing the road without checking for cars was not too dangerous a move. I was wrong. No sooner had I stepped off the curb than a loud horn blared and I found myself directly in the path of a banged-up blue sedan. Through the window, an older lady looked at me with a wry smile.

"You lost?" she asked, poking her head out the window.

"Was it that obvious?"

"Where you off to?"

"Well, that's a long story."

"An Englishman in Galesburg? I should think that story is long indeed. Try me."

I recounted my experience with the local rappers. She was enthralled by my journey across America and I saw the wheels spinning in her mind—I knew that look: "How can I help this poor chap?" I'm not sure if she felt guilt for nearly running me over but she seemed to want to help me along my path. Her first attempt was to offer me twenty dollars for dinner.

"It breaks my heart and disappoints my stomach, but I must decline."

She changed her tack and came up with another idea. (Only thing better than generosity: *persistent* generosity.)

"Okay, wait a minute there, I got it. My husband wouldn't look kindly on me picking up some strange man and giving him a ride, but my son is in the neighbourhood. He can do it."

A quick phone call and her son was on his way. As we waited, I found out the lady's name was Prue and she had lived in Galesburg most of her life. Soon her son Bob wandered down the street, a forty-something chap with a completely bemused look on his face.

"Hello, Mom."

"How was writing class, dear?"

"Good. But I can't say I was sad to be interrupted."

They kissed lightly and Bob turned to me.

"So you're the Englishman."

"I am indeed. Your mother has been quite kind to me."

"Ah, you got the accent and everything. Very cool. What do you say, Mom?"

"I say you take this $20 and go buy Leon some dinner. I think you two will get along just fine."

"You got it. Leon. My truck's this way."

We were soon heading to a local diner where I found my way to a little slice of heaven: the all-you-can-eat buffet.

If you've never been to an American all-you-can-eat buffet, I can only say this: it is a veritable smorgasbord. I had never seen anything like it, and have not seen anything like it since. You just grab a plate, and dive in: salads, steamed veggies and grilled veggies, and meat of a thousand varieties, assorted breads, and a dessert table that distracts even the most disciplined. When it comes to plate filling time, there are a dozen stations to visit. It's understood you'll eat an entire plateful, and then return to the buffet, grab a new plate and continue once again. How many times you do this is up to you. It's certainly a phenomenon that can be attributed to American abundance and even hospitality. But something tells me it might also be connected to the epidemic of obesity. But say what you will: it is distinctly American in its bigness.

In the middle of my third plate, I settled into a long confab with Bob. The man was a genuine Midwesterner, with a deep love for his family, and a proud member of his community. Our dinner conversation was centered on my trip but we soon started discussing his passion for connecting with people. It became apparent why he had been so eager to help. He was an adventurer in his own right and yearned to enjoy life to the fullest. He began telling me a daring story where he had found himself stranded in a Florida swamp with an ominous stranger. Now here was something I could relate to.

"I'm hitchhiking from North Carolina down to Florida. I'm going through Georgia and I look up and there's an old man in a company patrolling truck waving at me to get in. I'm nineteen years old, so I get up there. He says 'throw your bag in the back and I'll take you as far down as I am going'.

"He says, 'Whenever I come into town here or I make this run, I always go and see my uncle. You don't mind if we go and stop by there, do ya?'

"I said, 'Free ride . . . sure; it's cool.' Oh, the exuberance and ability to throw caution to the wind of a nineteen-year-old!"

I laughed, totally identifying.

"So, we get off the main road: from a four lane to a two lane, then from the two lanes to a one lane—paved—and then he turns, and we're on a one lane dirt road with trees hanging over and it's, you know, sort of swampy looking and we're getting back in the country and I'm thinking . . ."

"What have I done?!" I interjected.

Bob laughed. "Exactly! 'What have I gotten myself into?' You know it was like a total reverse thought. Now I know what fear is, what individuals think about. We pull up to this house and there are like twelve cars out front and he goes: 'Hey, he's not there.' I said 'He's not there?' And he says, 'No, his car is not here.' I said 'Well, whose cars are these?' He says, 'Oh, they are his, too. But the one he likes to drive isn't here so . . . '"

I was now fully expecting Bob to be fed to the crocodiles as his new friend turned on him revealing his psychotic side. Fortunately for Bob this was not to be. "So we turned around and left. He dropped me off. We were at this little roadside mom-and-pop store with old wooden floors, he took me in there bought me a drink and a sandwich and handed me two bucks. 'This is all I got left, take it. Get yourself down to your grandmother's.' I said, 'I can't take your money.' He said 'No, it's a gift, you can't refuse a gift.'

"So I took the money and went on down to Florida. Does he remember me to this day? Probably not, but I definitely remember him."

"That's the way it is: a sense of danger and generosity intertwined," I said.

"You got it," said Bob. "That's why we do it, though, isn't it?"

Bob was explaining what I had been feeling all along, potential dangers lurking at every corner, mixed with potential miracles. I was forced to trust the people who helped me, and they had to have a large dose of trust and faith in my intentions as well. Who knew where these interactions would end up? In today's modern society we tend to be awash with fear about our surroundings. I know that I have been guilty of this. Our fast-paced information-based society inundates us with stories of murders, abductions, and senseless acts of random violence. In response, we shut down. Shutting down creates an illusion of safety. I have realized that it's only an illusion. Trust is a rare commodity that only sporadically extends beyond immediate family ties. But when we risk, we discover we are all kindred spirits, floating along the same path.

"So," said Bob, tucking into a piece of apple pie, a generous scoop of ice cream on the side. "You need a place to stay."

"Yes, that is definitely my most immediate need."

"Well, I think we can probably provide that for you."

"Are you serious?" I responded with a grand smile stamped across my face.

"I just have to make a phone call. Because, as we know, there are only two rules in life, and rule one is keep the women happy."

Bob took out his cell phone and called his home.

"Hi. Is mom home yet?" I guess one of his children had picked up. "Can your dad have a houseguest tonight?" I could only imagine what the person on the other end of the phone was thinking. "A gentleman from England. Yep. He's got the accent and everything."

Bob lived in a comfortable home in a suburban area of town. Elegantly furnished, cozy, and clean. In the living room, he showed me an album of his reenactment photos. He was a member of a Civil War club that, throughout the year, performed reenactments of famous battles. Handing me two photos of himself with other actors in costume, he said I could keep them as a souvenir of my trip. He also promised that the next day he would let me dress up in costume and teach me how to throw axes.

"How to throw axes? Throw axes where? At who?" I asked. "And . . . why?"

"Leon! Every man ought to know how to throw an axe!"

I thought about this for a moment, and eventually agreed that he was right.

When I woke the next morning, Bob was true to his word and handed me a costume to wear. I tried to wriggle my way out of the indignity but he was insistent. No costume, no axe throwing! I caved in and soon found myself dressed up as a mountain man. The fun and games could now begin. Soon I found out what he meant by "throwing axes."

First, they were not axes. They were tomahawks.

In his backyard, Bob demonstrated how to throw a tomahawk. It's not as easy as it sounds. It took several tries before I could do anything remotely resembling a successful tomahawk throw. With practice, I somewhat mastered the art of tomahawk throwing and was having a grand old time. One of my efforts missed the target and landed closer to Bob than to the tree. He gave me a friendly glare and then spent a further ten minutes on "Tomahawk Throwing 101." Bob was definitely pulling out all the stops to make my respite in Galesburg enjoyable. Who would have thought I would have ended up here? It was only the previous evening that I was rapping and now I was throwing tomahawks at trees. Welcome to my new world!

Bob had a fatherly presence about him. He warmed up to me and we were finding ample things to connect about. He had two young daughters and I think the fact that there was some male energy in the house energized him. He also seemed to understand why I needed to get out of the stifling pressure of my previous life.

As the tomahawk throwing fest came to an end, Bob offered to take me for breakfast. We were joined by his wife and mother, whom I thanked several times for getting this whole adventure started. She had been magnificent. As we finished breakfast Bob decided to take his generosity to a new level; he wanted to find a way of getting me to Denver.

"From what I understand, a one way ticket is ninety-nine dollars and I have just been talking with the restaurant owner in there. She knows you can't take money, but she can donate ten dollars toward your ticket. And, I think I know enough people that we can raise the money to get you to Denver between now and five o'clock."

"You mean, a citywide collection?"

"Let's just say it's friends helping friends."

"Well, I . . . I mean if, if you . . . I mean, yes! That's just beyond, beyond all understanding but I mean if that . . ." he gently cut me off.

"The people of this community are very generous so I'm sure we can make this thing happen for you."

"Can I give you a hug?" I was ecstatic.

Bob just laughed as I embraced him and then kissed his

mother. Bob was going to collect the money and actually purchase the ticket to Denver.

His offer to elicit the help of an entire town was exceptional. The trip had never failed to amaze me, but this was one for the books. I was about to find my way further west with the help of an entire town. The feeling of gratitude was palpable. I had my suspicions about whether he could raise the $100 for my ticket, but he had no doubts. He was adamant that the little town of Galesburg was going to come up trumps.

Bob certainly seemed to know everyone and left no stone unturned in his bid to create a powerful wave of generosity. He was a fundraising machine, and I was pleasantly amazed to see doctors, car dealers, and insurance brokers hand over fistfuls of bills on my behalf. Apparently, Bob had a stellar reputation.

The day flew by as Bob and I drove around town in his trusty pick-up truck, squeezing out the generosity of the good folk of Galesburg. With the final dollar bill in hand we made our way to the station where Bob purchased the ticket on behalf of the town of Galesburg. As I stood on the tracks ready to board the train, I looked at Bob, his mother, his wife, and a handful of the townspeople who had some leisure time to meet me for my farewell. I hugged Bob and when I pulled away he kept his hand on my shoulder and looked me in the eye.

"Rule number two, Leon," he handed me my backsack, "be a friend."

9

Welcome to the Wild, Wild West

Modern man is the missing link
between apes and human beings.

—*Anonymous*

As my journey stretched from east to west, I was noticing something: I wasn't the only one looking for a helping hand along the road. Itinerants gravitate toward each other, and form a kind of fluid community on the open road. I was learning to embrace the idea of reciprocity: I receive *and* I give. On the road, I'm in a relationship with the world, that demands and takes what is given, and I give what I can.

I had just stepped on the train to Denver when a disheveled thirty-something woman sat down beside me.

"Where are you going?" she asked.

"Denver. How about you?"

"Salt Lake City. But, you know, via Denver."

I had been hoping to take a nap, but she was clearly yearning for someone to talk to. It was, I thought, the least I could do after all I had just experienced, to offer her my ear.

"I'm Christine," she said. "What's your name?"

"Leon, from London."

Initially, we started chatting about her kids, which put a gleam of light across her face.

"What are their names?" I asked.

"Heidi is the little girl, she is twelve, and Johnny is the little boy, he is nine. The most beautiful kids that have walked the earth."

Then, silence, and clearly deep sadness.

"Are you okay?" I asked.

She began to cry, but tried to sniff back the tears. "There is a man in the house with my children," she began, before breaking down again. "He has a gun."

"A gun?!" I asked. "What? Why?"

"He won't let me see them . . ." Her ex-husband was holding her children hostage from her—and this was only the beginning.

"When we went back to the domestic violence shelter because of it, they told me I needed to do a drug test and I told her, I said, you know what, it is going to come out positive. I do know that because I did *do* something because he had a gun right there and told me if . . . He held it right at me and told me if I didn't do this he would know that I was a police officer and that I would die and I was honest and I told everyone what I had done."

Christine was a little jumbled but she was claiming that her ex-husband had forced her to take drugs at gunpoint. And now she was about to fail a drug test at the very shelter she went to escape from him. Things were about to get worse as the inevitable positive test materialized.

"They were looking at me as being abusive to my children. I have made mistakes, but I love my children more than life itself."

"So the failed drug test at the shelter meant you lost custody of your children?" I asked.

She nodded, and brought a tissue to her nose. "When I was in Utah I had a restraining order against my husband and my restraining order expired in October. I was supposed to go to court which I had every intention of doing but I was afraid my husband would find me and my children."

"Wait," I said. "So you've been on the run?" She nodded again. "So . . . going back to Salt Lake City to fight for custody of your children—this is a major risk."

She continued. "I called my mom one day and I said, 'You know what . . . I said I really need you.' She suggested that I come back to Illinois, get my restraining order done, then she would help me get a lawyer and that Utah would not come and get my children as a result of me not going to court, as long as I had done everything I needed to do in Illinois and I believed her, she's my mother, you know. She said that she'd called people and checked and everything else and I believed her.

"They came to pick up my children Thursday night. My children were sent back to Utah. They were sent back because I didn't go to court and I didn't reply to the summons. If I don't get back to Utah by Thursday my children will be stuck in the system because they are going to look at it and say I didn't make an effort."

Outside, the light blue sky of Galesburg had deteriorated into a muggy dark black haze. Night had enveloped the train, as though Christine's story had invited the darkness. We talked for a few minutes more, and she offered me a granola bar from her bag. We nibbled in silence, and eventually I saw that she had drifted off to sleep.

It was time to try and get some sleep of my own. But, a young lesbian couple in the seat in front of me had different plans. They had started the trip in New York to start a new life together, and were bouncing their way by train to San Francisco, where a world of blissful romance and love-making by the sea awaited them. Unfortunately, judging by their constant bickering, I felt that the chances of matrimonial bliss were about as likely as me becoming a Nigerian sheep herder. Not to belittle Nigerian sheep herders, of course. I'm just not cut out for it. The war began soon after I had given up on the idea of getting any sleep.

"You're a fucking, lying bitch," the blonde murmured.

"What did you say to me?"

"Deaf as well. Why didn't you tell me about this before?"

"You never asked me, and anyway it's none of your business."

It seemed that they were arguing about one of them having had an "experience" with a boy a few years prior to meeting each other. The topic was not a civil one.

"None of *my* business? Then whose business is it?"

Things were getting a little out of hand. Literally. Food had just been thrown.

"I don't even know why I am coming with you!" the

blonde screamed just before the sandwiches started to fly around the cabin.

"I am going to sue you for assault!"

"For a sandwich?!"

Food was only the beginning. Now hair was being pulled and eyes jabbed.

As I've said, I'm a pacifist. But sometimes, well, you just gotta jump right into a lesbian fight. I placed myself in between them and demanded they both calm down.

"Ladies, please! You are going to get yourself thrown off the train!"

"I'm gonna fucking kill her!"

"No, you're going to kill me accidentally! And that would make my mother very sad. Do you want to make my mother sad?"

She relaxed, which I took as a no. Another passenger offered a seat that would keep the feuding females away from each other. The cabin was electrified, and I suggested calming the situation down by taking one of the ladies to the front of the train to drown her sorrows in whisky. I sat with the blonde and listened to all of her pent-up frustrations. After about thirty minutes they seemed to have calmed down enough to be in close proximity to each other *without* coming to blows. I settled back into my seat, keeping a watchful eye on the fragile cease-fire in front of me, putting to bed any fantasy I may have ever had of becoming a couple's counselor.

I did finally manage to get a few hours sleep and to my surprise when I awoke the two lesbians were best buddies and everything was going along swimmingly. Just before noon, the train finally reached Denver, approximately sixteen hours after I had left Galesburg. I said my good-byes to Christine, and watched her walk away; her shoulders slumped under the weight of the tough assignment awaiting her in Salt Lake City. I waved casually at my two lesbian friends heading down the road outside the main terminal, and turned into a pub that opened early. Generous Julie had given me the number of a friend of hers named Tom, so I decided to give him a call and see if he could help me out.

There was no answer. I waited another thirty minutes before trying him again, still no answer.

What to do? I hung out at the bar for a few hours, chatting with the locals who were coming and going, drinking, laughing, talking, slapping each other on the back. Not a bad way to spend an afternoon, even if all I could afford was soda water.

I called Tom one last time mid-afternoon, and fortunately this time he picked up. Explaining who I was and that I was calling at Julie's suggestion, he informed me that she had told him I may call and he agreed to come and get me. As he pulled up to the curb a half hour later, I was waiting and jumped in the passenger's side. He drove to a suburb with magnificent views of the Rocky Mountains. His wife and daughter, Andi, met us at the door. They showed me through their beautiful home to the guest room. It was an amazing house, by far the best I had stayed in all trip.

While Tom and his wife cooked dinner, I read to Andi, enjoying the family time I was again afforded on this trip. After a warm, comforting meal, I helped Andi bake brownies. Fortunately no one was poisoned. Though I couldn't eat any of the treats, it was pleasant to see the family enjoying my paltry efforts.

I found my way to bed early. As I put my head on the pillow I started to ruminate. I felt humility. I realized I would never be this far across America if it weren't for the goodness of people I had met only briefly. Their time, money, and assistance had carried me. Somehow they believed in me when I didn't or couldn't believe in myself.

I had done what little I could to aid them in return, sometimes simply listening to people whom others ignored. Listening is good medicine for those who feel alienated by society. Whilst on this journey, I found that I could relate to the downtrodden, the abandoned, the emotionally-bankrupt of society. For their sake as well as mine, I had to keep on going. I looked out at the darkening sky as the stars winked on, falling asleep gradually.

The next morning I woke up feeling sprightly. Over breakfast, I discussed my plans with Tom. Should I go south, maybe to Roswell, New Mexico? I had always been fascinated by the stories of aliens that emanated from that town. After some discussion Tom suggested I should head for Trinidad, Colorado.

"Now there's an American town," said Tom, as his wife slapped his arm playfully.

"Why Trinidad?"

"Sex change Capitol of the world!" said Tom.

"Tom! Not in front of Andi!"

Andi giggled.

Tom offered to drive me to a local gas station where I could find a ride to Trinidad, and I said my farewells to the beautiful house and warm hospitality. The station was heavily trafficked, but everyone was going north; Trinidad was south. As the truck-stop parking area cleared, I spotted a motorcycle on the far side. Dragging my feet, I made an approach to ask a Hell's Angel biker for a ride. After exchanging names, my new acquaintance offered to drive me north—sans helmet—to the next gas station that was more likely to have southbound traffic. Oh, the vagaries of life on the road . . .

The Angel was a real gentleman, not very talkative, but friendly enough. He dropped me at the gas station and refused any offer of payment. The station was servicing several travelers fueling their vehicles. I eyed a driver in a red corvette, figuring he might have the time and the means to take me along, and strode confidently to his door.

"Excuse me, may I ask you a very strange question?"

"Sure" he said, perplexed. "I suppose."

"May I buy your car?"

He laughed. "It is a beauty, isn't it?"

"It is. I want to buy your car for five dollars."

He stopped laughing for a moment, then started again. "You want to buy it for five dollars?" he asked increduously.

"Yeah, unless you'd take four?"

"Well, it's worth a little more than that . . ."

"I've got five dollars, and that's all I'll have for some time. But, if you want, I can tell you a really good story."

"Okay."

"I tell it better in a car, on my way south," I hinted, smiling.

He laughed again. I liked this guy already. "I'm going to Colorado Springs," he said. Any interest in joining me?"

"Is it south?"

"It is."

"Then get ready for a story!" I hopped in, we sped off, and I started from the beginning.

Robert laughed the best laugh and listened to my tales of pimps and rappers and friendly midwestern towns and my hopes for Hollywood. Then I turned to him.

"Your turn, Robert. Your story."

"That's a long one, too, full of a few twists as well."

"I listen well in a car traveling south."

He laughed and started in. From a military family, he was a military man. Retired now—honourably discharged—but thinking about it every day.

"If you were now in the army, would you be in Iraq?" I asked him.

"Yes."

"Is your unit in Iraq?"

"Yup. Six of them have been killed this year. The others come home in four months."

He grew silent. And I waited, not wanting to push too many buttons. After a while, I said softly, "I'm sorry about that."

"Yeah," he said, "me too." After a pause, he'd turned a corner in his mind. "You may not care, I dunno, being from London and all. But people here think we're over there trying to free the citizens from a dictator. We're just over there trying to get the rest of that oil. And that's coming from a soldier. We're mercenary soldiers at that. We're not defending our country. We're preserving an American sphere of influence in the Middle East, that's about it. And, as soldiers, we're getting paid to pillage a third world nation."

"You're not the only one who feels disappointed with how it all went down," I said.

"I know. But seems we don't have a say. And when you're asked to go, and told it's for your country, you go, no questions asked. Now that I'm out, I feel an obligation to tell people that I don't think it's right. And I never really did."

We were closing in on Colorado Springs, as I had seen numerous signs counting down the miles, so I told Robert that he could drop me anywhere convenient. He pulled over at a gas station just before the city and I told him I appreciated what he'd done, and what he'd said, even if he felt the two didn't match.

"We all do what we have to, you know?" he said. "Then later, we do what we want."

I shook his hand, waved farewell, and looked up to find myself at a gas station that seemed to have stepped out of a 1950s television commercial, complete with the old-fashioned gas pumps and an attendant with a bowtie. Andy Griffith might have been inside popping the top off his glass bottle of Coca-Cola.

An older gentleman with a kind, open face was finishing up washing his windshield when he spotted me and smiled. "Nice day, isn't it?"

"It is," I agreed. "I wonder, if an Englishman were to approach you and ask for a ride south, what might you say?"

"I'd say, you betcha. But he'd have to ride on the trailer."

I looked back at the trailer, which seemed to be about ready to collapse into a pile of metal, drug along behind a gleaming red pick-up.

He saw the look on my face and laughed. "Ha! I'm joking. Hop on in the cab!"

John was riding down south with his wife and youngest daughter. The family turned out to be devout Christians with a proud military tradition.

"I just had quite a conversation with a frustrated former military man. Seemed rather displeased with the Iraq situation."

"Yes, well, there's a lot of that going around. We try to see their point of view, but it's hard when you know you're doing the right thing."

I have always had a fascination with the military way of life: the sense of order, the courage, the purpose, the honor—all traits that I aspire to. I now found myself in the perfect situation to chat with someone who could enlighten me as to *why* men and women fight. What creates the situation for people to leave their families and risk their lives for their country? Prior to meeting John I spent my time thinking soldiers were just pawns of big government. Robert had kept this point fresh in my mind. But here was a guy who seemed completely ingrained in the military way of life, I was certain he could explain the reasons why people dance with the ultimate sacrifice. His answers were simple yet profound.

"Life is not fully lived if one does not give back, and to live for something greater than yourself is the sweetest of experiences. During my fighting days I had many reasons to leave home and go far—reasons far greater than myself."

"What was your toughest moment?"

"No question, without hesitation I can answer: fighting Saddam Hussein's Republican Guard at the infamous Battle of Medina. I was a tank commander; my responsibilities were the troops under my command. Protecting them from harm while successfully defeating Saddam was my main concern. At those moments I really felt my life secondary in importance to bringing those soldiers back home safely."

His presence struck a chord. I had spent most of my life living only for myself, never able to fully grasp the concept of being driven by something greater than myself. My life had seemingly been consumed by my own pettiness. That is why shame coursed through my body. It was a shame that, up to this point, my life had been practically meaningless. There was nothing I could point to with pride. John was mirroring a different way, one that appealed to me; a way of life where we find something to fight for. Not necessarily in the arena of battle, but something that is greater and more important than the mundane daily existence that can quietly consume us. Those who have found that are exceptionally lucky. They are the ones who create change in this world. I wanted to be one of those people. Driving through the hills of southern Colorado I had to accept that *I* was not one of them—yet.

Here I was, traveling in a car with a US Army veteran who had put his life directly on the line in pursuit of ridding the world of a tyrant. He had risked death and obliterating the fabric of his family. Here was a man who had courage written all over his face—a man of honor and substance. Looking into his eyes I felt the presence of a fearless warrior; a warrior who found a way to fight through his fears and serve a higher purpose. He was a role model for an improved way to live. I had been selfish, inward, and less than humble.

So far, I had failed to find something greater than myself to latch onto. I had always wandered around aimlessly, directionless, and certainly devoid of purpose. John was a perfect example of someone who had found purpose and lived it.

Above all I was fascinated by a single question: What did John possess that I didn't? How did he find his raison d'etre? Little did I know that as night would later fall, my chat with John would light the fuse for the kind of change I had always sought.

We stopped off for lunch at Subway and they fed me—always a welcome gift. I received the honor of being included in their prayers for the day.

"We thank you for this food, we thank you for bringing Leon into our lives, and getting him across the state; our thoughts are with our president, our soldiers, and our son-in-law Gerald in Iraq. God help them with the decisions they'll have to make today. In the name of Jesus. Amen."

After my ride with Ashley, I'd come to have a new perspective on American Christians.

As we continued down the road, we were still a while out of Trinidad so there was plenty of time for John to recount his more jovial military stories; stories that showed the lighter side of military life—the side that invokes the traveling spirit so vaunted by the high-cost commercials we see on our television screens.

Of course, the TV commercials never focus on the foreign food. John was grinning as he brought it up: "I had different foods I had never eaten before. I had *begogy*."

"Wow. Lebogy?"

"No, begogy."

"Oh," I said, and paused. "What's that?"

"Well, I am not entirely sure. It seemed like a beef dish, but sometimes I wondered if it was. Some of the guys said it might have been mispronounced, and was actually *kegogy*."

"Oh," I paused again. "But what's that?"

He looked at me and smiled. "Dog!"

I swallowed. "Seriously?"

He chuckled. "Oh, I dunno. That's what they said."

"Well, that's not the kind of thing they report on CNN. Army guys eating dogs."

"CNN! Pshaw. Commie News Network. Crap is what it is."

"Oh, yeah? What do you watch for news then?"

"You kidding? FOX, man. FOX all the way."

As we entered the sleepy town of Trinidad, it was dusk, the shops were closed, and the streets eerily silent. The journey with John was nearing its conclusion. I thanked him and his family. He let me out near the downtown area and I began walking through the town's center, hoping there would be a kind soul waiting around the corner with a kind word.

I was not to be so lucky.

The only places open were a few Wild West–type bars sprinkled with haggard looking men who seemed like they had not seen the light of day for years, huddled around their whisky shots. It did not bode well for finding some generous spirit. I decided against asking them for help. I felt that I had been transported to the days of Jesse James where one misplaced look would lead to a shootout in the town square. Trying to find a place to stay was probably going to be easier outside.

I walked around and stumbled across what I thought was a male construction worker. I asked him a simple question.

"Are you a man?"

"Sorry, what did you say? Am I a man? Why, do I look like a woman?" he asked.

"I have been told this town is the 'sex change capital of the world' and I just wanted to make sure that you were indeed a man."

"I am 100 percent man. What can I do for you?" he said smiling.

"I am looking for the mayor; do you know where I can find him?" I had spontaneously decided to revisit my plan of staying with a genuine American mayor. My last try in Galesburg had failed so miserably, I was hoping this attempt would be different.

"The mayor of Trinidad, I didn't even know there was a mayor of Trinidad, but you may be able to ask the police they should know."

The police—*again?*

He gave me directions to the station and off I went apologizing to him if my offbeat comments had offended him.

"You ain't the first person that's come to this town and played that gag!"

That shut me up.

I hurriedly walked a mile or so, finally finding the police station. Only problem: it was closed! Not only was the town deserted, but the police station was closed. How could this be? How can you have a town with a police station that is closed? I was baffled. Desperate, I tried to figure out what else would be open at this time of night. Trinidad was a small town, so my expectations were low. Noticing the lights of a public building a few blocks away, I walked over to find the city library, which was still open. Police protection wasn't available, but the collected works of J. K. Rowling were. Funny.

A reserved, tired-looking young woman at the front desk greeted me wearily.

"Can I help you?"

I told her about my quest to cross America through the kindness of strangers and my desire to meet the mayor of this leafy town. Her eyes softened, but she remained distant.

"I'll check with our head librarian," she informed me, heading towards her desk to call someone in another office.

A few minutes later a tall, slender man with light brown hair approached. We exchanged greetings and I let him know my situation. Serious, scholarly, and soft-spoken, he was the archetypal librarian. To my absolute astonishment,

Sean had lived in London for many years. He had lived in Kensington, only a few miles from the street where I had grown up.

"Here I am in the middle of nowhere—"

"Careful," he said jovially.

"Right, well, the middle of *Colorado* at least, and my path crosses with a man who lived just down the road from me. Surely, you, as an upright former resident of my beloved country can help me find the mayor or aid me in finding a place for the night?"

"I actually know the mayor quite well. Have a seat and we'll give him a call."

As Sean placed the call, I sat patiently in the library, embracing the quietness and tranquility that tends to fill such places. I looked at the rows and rows of books—Hemingway and Shakespeare and Faulkner and Neruda and a thousand others whose stories have shaped our common experience of the world. I wandered over to the nonfiction section, looking for one title in particular. I stopped at the Gs and scanned the stacks. The book I'd hoped to see wasn't there. In the place of Che Guevera's *The Motorcycle Diaries,* there was an empty space. Someone had checked it out. Someone, perhaps at this moment, was reading it. Someone, perhaps, just like me, would find the inspiration in Che's story to leave the small life they were trapped in and search for the larger world, and the larger country of their own mind. I smiled, and slipped my hand into the space. Now I was where Che had been; the journey that was his was now mine, and the transformation he felt I, too, was feeling.

I slipped my hand out of the space and walked to the end of the aisle. In front of me was a map of the United States, and I looked at Colorado. I was more than halfway to Hollywood. My trip, it just dawned on me, could be over soon.

What then?

I looked back down the aisle at the empty space where Che's great memoir had rested, and thought for the first time about the future. Che had his journey, expanding his worldview, and returned home to change the world. What was I going to do with my epiphanies, my revelations, my freedoms?

I was going to move to Los Angeles.

It struck me, with no sense of reason attached. I'd never even been to Los Angeles—and frankly there was no guarantee I'd make it there soon. Why would I live there?

But why not? Why go back home? What was waiting for me there? Boredom, mediocrity, and nothing much else.

In Los Angeles, I saw a chance to recreate myself in the image of all the experiences I had had during this trip. It offered newness and possibility. I wanted to make a difference in people's lives, even if a small one. I wanted to write about my experiences. I wanted to create meaningful entertainment for the masses. I wanted to bring a smile and a sense of purpose to the lives of others. I have always felt like a free spirit, one that was caged in the rarified world of business and finance. Expressing myself through television and writing was one way that I could get my point across to people and hopefully inspire them to change their lives for the better or at least spend a moment asking themselves pertinent questions about life. These were things I had always wanted to do, and there in L.A., perhaps, I would find the opportunity to actually do them.

With a reminder of John's wisdom and sense of purpose coursing through me, I realized everyone has it within them to create greatness in their own lives. Here was my chance.

The seed had been planted. For the first time during the trip I could see the proverbial light at the end of the tunnel. A new existence was within sight. I was not clear about how my transformation would take shape but I could sense its possibilities. I could taste it.

"Well, Leon." I spun around to see Sean, walking toward me, adjusting his glasses. "I'm afraid the mayor is out of town, but I've left a message with his son Joe. Until he calls back, why don't we take you to a small motel run by a group of Londoners? Just outside the city."

"Fellow Londoners! With a motel in Trinidad, Colorado? Brilliant!"

"Well, it's not as impressive as anything in Kensington, but you'll find it sounds like home at least."

"Good enough for me."

The motel was a twenty minute ride from downtown, and it was all I could do to stay awake for the journey. Sean's choice of Gregorian chants for background music didn't help. By the time we arrived, Sean offered to buy me a quick bite, but I had to decline.

"I'm on my last legs, but how about breakfast tomorrow?"

"It's a deal, but we'll have to meet at seven. Okay?"

"Okay. If I'm not up, come pound on my door!"

Despite my exhaustion, I sat on the bed thinking about my revelation at the library. I was literally in the middle of nowhere, staying at a roadside motel courtesy of a librarian who took pity on me and paid for my room, thinking about moving to a city I'd never seen and didn't even know when I'd reach. I fell asleep, either from exhaustion or the sheer desire to dream.

The next day dawned early, and Sean arrived by seven and took me to breakfast at Denny's. Over eggs, bacon, pancakes, and coffee, he promised to help me get in touch with the mayor's son, Joe, who worked at a museum featuring Trinidad's history. (If I couldn't connect with a mayor, I supposed meeting his son would be the next best thing.) Making a phone call, Sean set up our introduction and took me to the museum.

Joe was a virtual storehouse of information about the town—the geographical history, the political history, the mining history, the western trail of migrants in the mid–1800s. But Joe knew what I really was interested in.

"But I bet you've got one big question."

"Yes I do."

"Well, you've humored me by listening to all the history. Ask away."

"Sex change! How is *this* the sex change capital?"

Joe eased into it. "Though it appears very conservative, Trinidad has always had a gambling and prostitution side; it was certainly this way at the turn of the century. There used to be mafia people here, too."

"Yes, but why its current claim to fame?"

"Well, that all started with Dr. Stanley Biber."

He had come to Trinidad after serving in the Korean War. An unassuming man, he became the town's general surgeon, performing typical procedures up until about 1969, when a colleague whom he knew as a female, but was really a male, asked him to perform a surgery to make the gender switch. Knowing little about transsexual surgery, Dr. Biber learned all he could and performed the operation.

Joe explained in further detail: "In the seventies, Dr. Biber started the trend, pioneering the surgery, as at the time no one was really doing it. It helped that Trinidad isn't exactly on the beaten path, you know. Folks could fly in and out very discreetly. Nobody really knew that they were here. Biber did tons of them; particularly in the seventies. By the late eighties and into the nineties, other doctors came and set up shop. Soon, it had its name: The Sex Change Capital of the World. (But I actually I think it's Thailand now, because it is cheaper and easier). But people continue to come here. They're opening a bed and breakfast for transgender patients to recover after surgery. Trinidad just has had everything. Every kind of person, I think, has been here at some point."

"Even a lonely Londoner."

"Even that!"

Trinidad was, in essence, a home for those in transition. Here, hidden from the world, they could find a peace and anonymity unavailable in the larger cities of America. Trinidad gave them a place to recover and integrate their new gender into their lives and then go back and face the rigors of the modern world as stronger more rounded individuals. Trinidad was the place in-between.

And it was for me, too.

"So where to next?" Joe asked.

"What's nearby where I could catch a ride to?"

Joe thought for a minute. "Well, I think Susan's headed to Santa Fe today or tomorrow. Susan!" he hollered. She emerged from the back of the museum, a settled, middle-aged woman with a nametag that said Museum Director.

"Our curious friend Leon here is in need of a ride to your lovely vacation town of Santa Fe. Can you take him?"

"You bet! I hate that drive anyway. Keep me company, Leon?"

"I've got stories!"

And so it was agreed. I still had to find lunch and agreed to come back in about an hour for my lift. Feeling particularly hungry, I headed down the street to look for a restaurant. I finally got directions to a small local place where I offered to work for food. The owners agreed to bring me a chicken salad in return for forty-five minutes of dishwashing duty—the first "real work" I'd done since starting on my journey. One of the waitresses, who had been listening to my conversation with the restaurant owners, sat down beside me as I devoured my lunch.

"My shift's ending. Thought I might say hello."

She told me that she was on the run from her husband who was attempting to track her down.

"I fled Florida over a year and a half ago with my children. My ex-husband, before he deployed to Iraq, put my head through the wall in our bathroom—in front of our children. And they were going to let him come back into the house and I didn't want to be hurt anymore, so I left. We were in four domestic violence shelters for a year to get away from him, and then he found us here, in June. He kidnapped my daughter and took her back to Florida. While I was still here at the shelter, he had a woman pose as me in court in Florida and give up my parental rights. *My daughter is six!*"

Why was I finding this story so frequently—Cinnamon, Christine, and now this young lady? What was happening that these stories were being drawn to me? Or were they so common in America that one couldn't help but run into them? Whatever the case, I was disturbed, and only a little comforted knowing this strange fact: sometimes it is easier to talk to a stranger than anyone else in the world. My very status as an outsider, someone who would be here a little while, and then would move on, qualified me to be the recipient of such heart wrenching stories. People could unburden themselves to me without fear of judgment or consequence. In a few hours, they knew I would be on my way, never to see them again, and that fact opened up a safe space to share. The art of listening has been all but lost in this frenetic world we live in, but my trip had created in me an ability to sit and listen. Not to take anything, just to offer a silent place for people to let out their hopes and fears. This was enough for me in the moment and I sensed it was enough for this young waitress.

She never even told me her name.

At one point she felt she couldn't continue and our little impromptu heart-to-heart ended. I gave her a warm embrace and she found her way to the back room where the tears that had been welling up poured out. Another moment of compassion between two souls had come to life. Yet again, I was reminded about the real reason for this trip. I was searching for my true path in life but I was ultimately searching out the lost art of connection between people. I had so much to learn from all these wise souls. Each connection I made inspired in me the iron strength to find a way *never* to live the same way I did before this journey.

"Ready, Englishman?" asked Susan when I wandered back to the museum.

"I am."

"Then let's hit the road. Santa Fe's where dreams come true, you know."

I didn't know that. But I believed her.

10

Wolfdogs and Balloons

When love is not madness, it is not love.

—Pedro Calderon de la Barca

"Maybe I should call my mom," the teenage guy said, thinking aloud.

"Rule number one in life," I told him, echoing my friend in Galesburg, "Keep the women happy."

This made him smile, and I smiled back. I couldn't believe this might work.

Night had quickly descended on Santa Fe, New Mexico, and, with Susan's warm car and good conversation a fleeting memory, I was preparing myself for another night of possible trouble. During my journey, my emotions had swung so many times from total euphoria to total desperation, I was certain that my brain would implode. Every great experience of hospitality would inevitably end, leaving me wondering what would happen next, if I would find another kind soul in the wilderness. But every hopeless moment was always rescued by unexpected friends. I was never in either extreme too long.

But this was looking bad.

If Santa Fe was the place where dreams come true, as Susan had casually claimed, I was going to have to pull off an eleventh-hour miracle. Otherwise, the streets would be my bed.

Across the street from where I stood, I noticed a young couple. I waved at them as I approached. They seemed confused by my boldness but did not run. This was a positive sign: when they don't run from you. We talked a few minutes while I asked about the town and where I might find someplace to crash for the night.

Then I took a chance. I'd come this far, I thought, why not just ask them straight out about staying with them? I mean, we had already spoken for five minutes so we were practically related!

"Listen, how about I just stay with you tonight?" There you go, I did it.

They looked at each other blankly.

They were just kids, in their late teens at most. Probably shouldn't even be out this late, I thought. This meant I was probably going to have to speak with their parents to actually manifest this reality.

"Maybe I should call my mom," the teenage guy said, thinking.

"Rule number one in life," I told him, echoing my friend in Galesburg, "Keep the women happy."

This made him smile, and I smiled back. I couldn't believe this might work.

"Damn straight!" said his girlfriend. "I like you, Leon."

"My mom would probably be entertained . . . well, I don't know." He was thinking about his next move with the reality of this random Englishman's request ringing through his ears.

"Call her!" said the girlfriend.

"Hey, Mom. No, everything's fine. Sorry I woke you. So I'm down on the plaza, and there's this guy who's going around the country living on five dollars a day and he is asking me if he could stay at our house tonight."

I waited with bated breath as his mother digested her son's strange call.

"Dude. She wants to talk to you!" he said, handing me the phone quickly.

"Oh!" I said, surprised. "What should I say?"

"Dude, I don't know? Rule number one and all that."

"Right." The kid was smart.

"Hello. Yes, hi! That's right. Five dollars. Uh-huh. I'm happy to give you the five dollars, if you like. Yes, ma'am. . . ."

We spoke for five minutes, and I felt very proud of myself for somehow persuading her that I was genuine. And over the phone!

"I managed it!"

"Oh, she just likes your accent," said the girl. "His mom loves English accents."

The kids were Zev and Carrie. I hadn't really expected them to be able to help, as they were literally the first people I had met since the museum and they were probably under eighteen-years-old. But now I had a place to stay and the rest of the night free from worry.

Or so I thought.

With a warm bed sorted, I could focus on far less pressing matters such as what to eat. Zev and Carrie were on their way to a party, as it was Friday night. Since I was now their responsibility, I was going to be the guest of honor. They stopped and grabbed a pizza en route, and since my night's accommodations were secured, I tossed my money into the pot.

We picked up perhaps the largest pepperoni pizza I'd ever seen, and chowed down on our way to the party. The night appeared to be off to a soft and easy beginning. We wound our way through the streets of the city, across a maze of stucco and adobe style houses. Santa Fe is the epitome of artsy, and its charm twinkled under the bright desert stars.

But the opening salvo of the evening was misleading. The underworld of Santa Fe teenagedom was anything but a soft and easy place. The moment we stepped into the house party, the world became very strange. Very strange indeed.

The music was straight from an acid trip scene by Ken Kesey, and the lighting owed much to the aesthetic of Tim Burton. At a table in the corner of the living room, a man was bent over, counting the granules form a salt shaker open in front of him. People were dressed as genies, Arabian princesses, and belly dancers, all of them slinking across a New Age backdrop of bongos, Hindu chanting, palm reading, and more belly dancing. There was a constant flow of guests coming and going, each group, stranger than the previous. Yes, I was in Santa Fe. But I was not sure which side of town I had found myself in.

"Virgins!" a young woman screamed from the doorway. "Virgins!"

She was dressed in hardly any clothing, and wielded a large saber above her head. Yes, a *sword.* She walked into the main room and stood there silently, while all shouting ceased and drum-playing stopped.

"I am looking for virgins! A sacrifice must be made!" She stared about the room with a twisted smile on her face.

"Are there any virgins in the room?" she cackled.

Silence.

"Virgins!" she screamed. "Are you a virgin? You? You?" She looked at me. "*You?*"

I shook my head no, never more proud of my relationship history.

She made a few more manic cries for virgins to sacrifice, but it soon became evident that there were none, or if there were, they were not about to stand up and be chopped to pieces. The saber-wielding virgin-hunter seemed to run out of steam in her quest to find fresh blood. The music slowly started up again. Soon the house was back to full rumble.

Where the hell was I? How did I manage to find myself in this crazy situation? I placed myself in a strategic position in the house—the corner near the kitchen—where I could watch the unfolding events without drawing too much attention to myself, and perhaps make a quick exit out the back door if needed. A large, muscular black man playing a bongo very badly. Four white women belly dancing to the sound of djembe drums. A small group of people engaging in Hindu chanting. And the only conversation I managed was with a rather inebriated chap: "Every Friday night, I streak around campus wearing nothing but sneakers and an American flag."

"Really?" I replied, tempted to share my own story from my wild night among the frat boys in Charlottesville. I thought better of it.

"Yes. I find it the best way to support our troops. They are protecting my right to be naked, after all."

I wonder what Robert and John would have said to that.

Waves of people kept arriving, and each time I imagined the house to be full, more people crammed inside, as though it were expanding to welcome them. Maybe that's what the chanting was doing—effecting some kind of enchantment on this place.

"Eat, Leon!" cried Zev, who had spotted me in my corner. "Be merry!" He and Carrie motioned me toward the food.

I smiled and nodded. There was no way I was eating anything in this place. I began to wonder if this was the night I was destined for. Would Carrie and Zev leave anytime soon?

Then, I found a reason for them not to.

A girl, sitting calmly. Calmly! Dressed in jeans and a jacket, she seemed unaware of all the commotion. It was as though she had been placed there just for me, a kindred soul among the throbbing masses. She did not belong. Then again neither did I. Perfect.

I tentatively approached and asked how she was. She completely ignored me. I tried again. Still nothing. Then I noticed the earphones. She was listening to her iPod. I motioned with my hands to let her know that I was there and she took off her earphones.

"What are you listening to?"

"Mozart," she said with a small smile.

Little did I know that this brief conversation would stir my heart in places that I did not think possible. Do I believe in love at first sight? No, I don't. But I do believe there are people out there who you connect with on a far deeper level than with others—and sometimes that's immediate. This was one of those moments.

We sat in our little corner oblivious to the mayhem swirling around us and talked and talked. Katherine was her name, and she was an artist in Santa Fe, where she had come to fulfill her dreams.

"Dreams come true here, I've heard," she said.

"I heard the same thing today. Do you think it's true?"

"Maybe. Sometimes, yes." She smiled.

It was well past one—and the party was winding up instead of down. It seemed that the whole of Santa Fe had found its way to the gates of this house, and everyone had brought their closeted weirdness with them. It was getting practically impossible to talk with my new friend. I beckoned her to follow me outside. There was no way we could hear each other clearly in the uproar of the indoor celebrations.

The night was pitch black and endless; there was a mystical quality that had at first sparked fear, but now opened the door to exciting possibilities.

I remember the exact time for some reason. I looked at my watch, and the time froze in my mind: 2:07 a.m. Then I opened the door. It seems a normal thing to do, open a door.

Then came the wolfhound.

The homeowner's prized possession, a gorgeous wolfhound bounded through the open door, past me, and into the darkness. I spun around and ran as fast as possible into the dark street, Katherine right behind me, chasing the gray-furred blur into the night. We called and sang and whistled, attempting every trick to coax the animal back into our arms. We failed. I kept thinking how I would feel if some stranger whom *I hadn't even invited* to my house managed to let my beloved Boston terrier, Winston, roam freely in the dead of night. For all I knew there could be a gang of coyotes on the prowl for some fresh wolfhound meat. And I was providing dinner in the form of a beloved pet.

Katherine and I spent nearly an hour running around the streets of Santa Fe in a futile attempt to pin down the dog. We were tired, winded, sweaty, and depressed. Not surprisingly, the dog was evidently far smarter than we. And he was having a wonderful time evading capture.

"Let me introduce you to a little thing called the New Mexico shuffle." Katherine said, panting like the dog, winded from the run.

"Is that a dance?" I asked.

"Not exactly. You stay here."

She gave me her jacket and then surged ahead, trying to close in on the dog once and for all, darting first in one direction, then in another. Every time she got within a whisker of ending this adventure, our new friend would dart off into the night. And I was left laughing in the middle of the street, with the mountains standing stoic and still under the moon. A metal clang reverberated through the dark street, and I hollered for Katherine.

"He's in the Dumpster!" she yelled, as excited as she'd been if the ice-cream truck had rounded the bend with George Clooney passing out cones. She ran toward the metal box and, without pausing, leapt inside the dark and fragrant abyss.

"Katherine! Katherine—what the hell are you doing?" I called out, laughing.

I was in the middle of Santa Fe, in the middle of the night, chasing a woman who had just lept into the trash, in her chase after a dog, that was probably chasing a rat.

And I was having the time of my life.

After a few more frantic pleas for Katherine to confirm that she had not fallen down a ravine, there was still no answer. The Dumpster was situated in a field, and I was not even sure she had actually jumped into it.

She had disappeared.

For fifteen minutes I searched for her in the pitch darkness. Nothing.

It was decision time; did I follow her into the rubbish dump or go back to the house? I took the easy and probably shameful decision of returning to the house, without the dog and, most worryingly, without Katherine. Was I going to be blamed for her disappearance? Everyone saw me leave the house with her, and now I was returning to the house with only her jacket! What the hell would people think if she actually did fall in a ravine or disappear indefinitely? I could just see the headlines the next morning on the news wires:

British man questioned in
disappearance of local girl.

Prime suspect in Santa Fe
missing girl case arraigned.

Prosecutors ask for death
penalty in New Mexico case.

The simple truth was I had left the house with Katherine and come back without her. This was not good. Not good at all.

Zev met me at the door completely unaware of what had just happened with Katherine.

"Time to go," he said lightly.

I tried to stall him until she returned—hoping she would. I could not leave this party without knowing what had happened to Katherine. Would I ever see her again? At the same time I could not upset the person who was giving me a place to stay for the night. Finally, just as Zev was losing patience with me, Katherine came jogging toward us, seemingly in one piece.

I ran to her, yelling: "What the hell happened to you? I was worried!"

"Oh don't worry, all is well."

"But where did you go?"

"I jumped into the garbage area looking for the dog, but I couldn't find it so I just lay down and took a nap!"

"A nap? In a rubbish bin?"

"Yup!"

I had no desire to understand the night's events, only to revel in the happiness I'd found for that hour, and the knowledge that the girl who'd given me such free joy while running wildly in the New Mexico night, was just fine. I gave her a big hug.

"Okay then, we ready?" Zev asked.

"One last thing," I said. "Katherine, we have to tell the owner that the dog is gone."

"Oh right. Yes, that's true. We should probably do it together."

"Okay. Where is she?"

"Oh, you met her, I think," said Zev.

"Yeah?"

"Yeah. She's the one with the sword."

Shit.

I was to reveal to the saber-wielding hostess that I had lost her dog.

"Zev," I said, placing my hand on his shoulder. "If I should die in this adventure, I hope you'll carry my ashes to the Hollywood sign and scatter them across the ocean I shall never see."

"Dude. That was deep. Sure."

Katherine and I ventured back into the pulsating house, and found the belly dancing, virgin-sacrificing hostess. I cleared my throat.

"I am afraid that I have lost your dog. I accidently let it out and Katherine and I have spent the last hour or so trying to find it, but . . . it's gone." I waited for the sword to fall.

"My dog? I don't have a dog."

Katherine and I looked at each other, bewildered. "What, but I thought it was your dog . . ." Katherine said.

"A large wolfdog? Are you sure you don't have a dog?" I asked.

Then it all came back to her. "Ah yes, I do have a dog. That's right. Yes. Thank you. He always runs off. He'll be back." She took Katherine's hand and placed it on mine. "But you are so nice. Let me ask: are you virgins?"

We slipped away as quickly as we could, and Zev honked his horn from the street. "Hey," Katherine said, as I had turned to go. "That was fun."

"Fun? Yeah. That seems to not quite describe it. It was the best time I've had in a long time."

"So the balloon festival is tomorrow. In Albuquerque."

"Oh, yeah? I find that there are always happy people wherever there are balloons."

"That's right! So would you like to be happy with them?"

"I'm sorry?"

"Do you want to come with me?" she asked. "It's worth seeing, you know, before you leave."

I couldn't help but smile widely. "I'd absolutely love to, Katherine."

"Good," she said with that brief smile that was enigmatic and equally seductive.

Katherine arrived at five-thirty—not three hours after our chase of the wolfhound had begun—and we headed to the balloons and happiness.

"What's that in the back?" I asked. There were stacks of cloth and wood.

"Oh, some of my paintings."

"Oh, really? Can I—I mean, would you mind if I looked?"

"Umm. Sure. I don't really mind."

This girl was talented. She had drawn a picture of Superman that perfectly captured the man of steel's sense of invincibility. I held it in my lap in the front seat, and stared at it.

"Well? I can't tell what you think," she said in a small, sweet voice.

"I—I think it's amazing," I said, near tears. "I think it is exactly how it should be."

I looked at her and she looked back, smiling faintly. Here was a woman who was passionate about the direction her life was going. She was living her dreams. She had courage and passion.

Did I?

When you're confronted with the beauty of people who

have broken free of their own limitations, it reminds you how far you have to go. But if they can do it, so can you. I could still create my own destiny. I could still change things for the better. I could still create for myself a life that had purpose and meaning and that aligned with my creative instincts. I could still give back to people even if it was a small amount. I could still choose a new life.

"Katherine, let's pull over up here."

"Have to use the bathroom already, huh?"

"No, no. Something else. Just as pressing, though. Can I borrow your cell?"

"Sure," she handed it over. "Everything okay?"

I nodded as I stepped out of the car and dialed my father's number.

Straight to voicemail. As always.

I heard the beep and started speaking before I could talk myself out of it. I don't know if I made much sense—I felt like I was babbling and rambling—but I know I said enough. I know I said this: "I'm not coming back, Dad. I'm moving to Los Angeles. And I'm going to do what I know I should. I don't know what's going to happen, or how it's going to work, but I know that right now I feel more alive than I have in a long time, and I'm not about to give that up. I guess . . . I just wanted you to know."

I hung up, and looked out to the mountains, gray in the morning mist, the sun's first rays illuminating their peaks. The vast desert stretched out before them, and the thin stretch of road went on for miles and miles. Katherine had gotten out of the car and was leaning on the hood of the Chevrolet, looking as pretty as a girl has ever looked on earth. I shuffled toward her.

"Everything good?" she asked.

I leaned on the hood beside her. "You know what's on the other side of those mountains?"

"Desert?"

I smiled. "Yeah. That. And then there's Los Angeles. And the ocean. Just over those peaks."

"You ever been?"

"Nope." I answered. "Not yet. But when I get there, I'm going to paint a picture of Superman."

"Oh yeah? As good as mine?"

"No, never as good as yours. But it'll be my own."

"I hear you."

We sat there for a little while longer, watching the sun rise.

"To Albuquerque?" she asked, sticking an elbow gently in my ribs.

"You bet!"

"To the balloons!" she sang. We spun off into the road and gunned it. In an hour and a half, we were there.

Katherine told me a little about the history of the festival. I was fortunate to have found my way to New Mexico slap bang in the middle of a worldwide event. Each year nearly one thousand balloons are launched. She told me the sight is startling. On our approach we saw some of them ascend into the sky. We arrived and parked, and then began walking around the fairgrounds, looking at all the flat balloons, resting until their time to be lifted to the sky by fire.

Then they were off. A few here, then there, then everywhere. Dozens of them, in dozens of colors. Baskets of all shapes and sizes carrying individuals and groups. They floated across the sun and clouds, and people oohed and aahed like at a fireworks show.

"Amazing," I said, enthralled.

"I told you," Katherine said, elbowing me again in the ribs. "Pretty great, right? Balloons and happiness."

We stayed for hours, grabbed a bite, and then looked at the time. I knew it was coming—the time to say good-bye—but I'd refused to consider it until the last minute.

"Will you keep painting?" I asked.

"I can't *not* paint," she said. "It's what I do."

Looking at Katherine's bright eyes and serene face, I wished I could put her in my pocket and take her with me for the rest of the trip. Reaching into *her* pocket, she handed me a small plastic coyote. "Here," she said, putting it in my hand. "This will remind you of the wild dogs you encountered here."

"Thanks," I said, meaning for more than the coyote. She understood, and nodded.

A balloon blocked out the sun, and we both looked up as it moved toward the mountains, catching the light on its brilliant red fabric.

"It *is* where dreams come true," she whispered, then kissed me on the cheek, and ran back to her car. I slipped the coyote in my pocket, and turned to the open road.

11

Vacancy at the Bates Motel

I believe in getting into hot water; it keeps you clean.

—*G. K. Chesterton*

Katherine had been a bright light, a young girl whose soul was clear, and whose artistic outlook was refreshing—especially for one like me, who had been stuck in the corporate world far too long. There was something clean about her, and the moment I found it, I realized it was what I was seeking in myself: a purity of heart.

I hadn't embarked on the trip to create a love connection, but I was out to experience life in all its varying forms. Love being one of the main ways humanity expresses itself; I suppose I should have expected that at some point along the way, I might just . . . fall in love. It certainly wasn't something I had expected, but why not? I'd wanted openness;

I'd sought dependence and connection, and in its most radical form, it is love, partnership, and intimacy. The longer I thought about it, the more it became clear to me that what I was feeling for Katherine was a very good sign: I was becoming the person I wanted to be.

Flipping the tiny toy coyote over in my hand, I was reminded of a poem I had read by Indian poet Tukaram. I couldn't recall the exact lines—if only I'd had my cell phone!—so I had to settle for what I remembered as the main point. Tukaram reminds us that loving your neighbor the same way you love your dog will free you. I laughed when I thought of it, because, on my first encounter with this poem during college, I must admit to having been confused. What on earth was this man talking about? He may have been an enlightened being, but he was also evidently slightly confused.

My time with Katherine had unlocked the key to understanding the poem. What if I could transfer the love I felt for my little four-legged friend and shine the light of love in the direction of *people* in my life? It was a great moment coming to this realization. I had read the poem years before and here I finally *felt* the message.

That would stay with me, but Katherine was gone. And now I needed to find my way out of Albuquerque. I wandered from the parking lot back toward the fair, past vendors and games, weaving amidst the families and friends, and found myself in the classic car show. Dozens of perfectly painted, washed, waxed, shined cars spread out over the grassy field. I'd never really been a classic car fan, but these beauties would win anyone over. They were clearly nurtured and loved by some individuals committed to their upkeep. They were tokens of someone's love.

Whenever people are as enthusiastic about something—balloons, art, food, sports, whatever—as these people were about their classic cars, it's easy to start a conversation. Simply ask them to talk about what they love. Of course, I was hoping that, after some fun car talk, someone would take me toward California.

No such luck.

As friendly as they were, all the classic car owners I chatted with were staying over another day or heading in other directions. Seemingly no one could help me out, until, as always, from somewhere came a glimmer of hope.

A middle-aged guy wearing a checked flannel shirt and baggy pants with about a thousand pockets, suggested I check with the car show organizer, who he called "the head honcho." In my experience, if anyone can do something for you, head honchos can.

After several false leads, I finally located the boss, Michael, a tall, short-haired, clean-shaven fellow, with a habit of placing his hand on the shoulder of whomever he was speaking with. He was busily chatting with various car enthusiasts. After three or four attempts to get to him through the crowd, I finally made contact.

"You the boss around here?" I asked.

He continued signing a few papers in front of him. "That's what they tell me."

"Excellent. Well, head honcho, if you've got thirty seconds, I've got a story for you."

He looked up. "A story? Is it a good one?"

"That's what they tell me."

He laughed. "Okay, kid. Hit it!"

So in less than half a minute, I gave him the tale. My shortest retelling yet.

He crossed his arms when I finished. "Well, that sounds like a short story that has a long story behind it."

"You could say that."

"So if I want to hear the rest, what do I have to do? I mean, you weren't telling me that story for your health, right?"

I laughed. "Well, head honcho. I need a ride. Since the Hollywood sign is where I'm going, and I'm not there yet."

And there it was: his hand on my shoulder. "A ride for your story. Sounds like a deal. My boyfriend and I are leaving shortly, and we're heading due west. But bring some water: I want the story from start to finish. Meet me by the silver Cadi in half an hour."

I kept my feet on the ground, though I wanted to leap for joy. I spent three dollars on a corn on the cob, and half an hour later, I was standing next to the most pristine classic Cadillac I'd ever laid eyes on.

"Well, Leon. Whaddaya say?" Michael asked, approaching in long strides from the booth where I'd left him.

"I say, let's go!"

He laughed a deep, hearty laugh. "Leon? You ready?"

"Always! The road awaits!"

"Then let's not keep the road lonely and waiting," Michael said. "Go ahead, Leon. Take the wheel."

"Sorry?" I was astonished to have been offered the opportunity to drive this beauty.

"Come on, you Brits drive, right? I mean, you know, stay on the right side of the road and all, but come on. Drive and start that story."

I couldn't resist. Settling into the leather seats, I adjusted the side mirror, put my hands on the wheel and took us onto the road.

"Is this a'52?"

"Close—a '58," he corrected me.

We hit the open road, with the mountains behind us and the blue sky rushing up toward forever. What a rush. I couldn't stop smiling.

"Feel like James Dean?"

"Or James Bond!"

"My passion for cars is what brings me the most joy in life. Other than my time with Craig, who you're going to meet when we get home."

We drove along in silence for a while. "There's something spiritual about this, isn't there? Almost like you're driving in the past," I said.

"There is indeed a spirituality here. Most of the cars I have come out of a junk yard. And then, I bring them back to life."

"Resurrection," I said.

"You got it. That's my pleasure."

"How many do you have?"

"Oh, thirty-six in total, but they're all in different states of repair or restoration."

"What's the oldest car you have?"

"A 1940 Cadillac Series Sixty Special with the battery sunroof. As far as I know they only made six of them. Pull over here."

I relinquished the wheel, and settled into the passenger seat to hear Michael's stories. He was a fascinating guy who seemed to have found a real passion for life. I sensed it from his whole body language and cheery outlook. It's quite telling how people who have a raison d'etre and true passion have far better energy than those who don't. I have often been in the perilous state of low energy due to a total lack of direction. This was definitely not the case with Michael. There was a shining light emanating from deep within. I could feel it.

"What is it about the West?" I wondered aloud.

"Sorry?"

"Oh, nothing." But there was something about the American West. There was a reason people had kept migrating farther and farther west over the decades. It wasn't just for gold. Sitting next to Michael I felt a small vindication in having left my old life behind. I was now part of that long train westward, that large group that had left an easier world behind and taken a course toward the better, the harder, the more beautiful. And I could see in Michael's eyes what I was looking for, what I'd seen in Katherine. I sensed purpose and joy in him, a joy to which we are all entitled but that few of us actually acquire. "We all die," my grandfather had once told me while we sat upon one of those massive Greek rocks looking out over the sea. "But few of us live."

"And . . . ." said Michael, pointing ahead. "Here we are."

We'd arrived at a concealed yard filled with old cars. It seemed that Michael had taken a small detour instead of going straight to the house.

"This is my work lot," Michael said. "I've got to grab a few things, and I thought you'd like a look. This is, as you said, where the resurrecting happens." He smiled and slapped my shoulder and wandered off toward the garage.

I looked around at the endless variety of cars, each in a state of disrepair, or re-repair. It certainly looked less like Resurrection Central and more like Auto Graveyard. The empty tomb it was not. But miracles happened here nonetheless, I supposed. Who knew where one of these dilapidated units would be in five years? Perhaps Michael would be showing it off at a show, and using it to give a ride to some wanderer.

I ran my hand along the top of an old sedan that looked a great deal like my father's old car, the one he used to drive on the weekends when we'd head to the countryside. I imagined, for a moment, that this was that same car, that somehow had made its way across the ocean to say hello. As I was indulging in my fantasy, I was distracted by a disheveled looking guy, who was watching me silently from a few yards away.

"Hey, man."

"Hey there yourself. I work for Michael. You like that one?"

"Oh, this one? Yeah, yeah. Reminds me of my dad's old car, actually."

"So, you're the Brit—the madman traveling around relying on kindness."

"I see my fame has preceded me. Yeah, I am the one: Leon. Who are you?"

"Marco!" came back the reply. And a quick bear hug completed the proceedings.

As he pulled away, I realized the one fact I couldn't ignore about him: Marco had no front teeth. Not one. It turned out that he had had a losing argument with a shovel earlier in the week. Apparently he and his brother were digging a hole in a field. Why they were digging a hole, in the middle of the desert, I did not ask. But they were digging. And while they were digging, Marco's brother abruptly smashed him in the face with the shovel. Yes, that's right. Marco was smashed in the face with a shovel by his brother. I never found out if this was an accidental assault, or if Marco's brother had been digging the hole in the ground as the coup de grace for a long-term sibling rivalry; Cain meets Abel, Southwest-American style. I didn't pry too deeply. Anyway, if Marco had been on the other end of a botched murder attempt, he was obviously still standing, so things couldn't be too bad. This did of course, beg the question: where was Marco's shovel wielding brother?

After digesting Marco's unpleasant run-in with a shovel we got chatting about *his* journeys around the world.

"After your thirteenth year or so, you'd be tired of it, too."

"Really? You went traveling for thirteen years?" I asked wide-eyed. "That's a very long time to be on the road."

"Yeah. I've been a welder, carpenter, everything. Just went all over the country. Just trying to see it, you know, just go from one end to the other. Just working your way through it, you know what I mean. Got tired of traveling, ran a strip club for a while in San Morgan and I went down with it after my break up with the missus. About a year ago, I hit the road again and found Albuquerque. This is the greatest spot, I think, on earth right now. I wish you could stay longer—we'd get you drunk!"

"Oh, that's nice of you, but—"

"Seriously it's like a New Mexican tradition here in Albuquerque, you know. The highest DWI rate and everything else. If you don't get drunk here, man, you're not part of New Mexico. Everyone is trying to kick my butt for bringing that up but that's the truth, everybody I know always does it."

I certainly wouldn't hire Marco as the face of the tourism board for New Mexico, but maybe he did have a point.

"All right! Let's go!" Michael said, emerging from the garage with his boyfriend, Craig, in tow.

"Hey Leon, good to meet you." Craig said with a slight midwestern twang.

"It's a pleasure meeting you to."

"Marco, let him go, no time for beer tonight!" Craig teased.

Marco waved good-bye as we sped off down the road. Michael, Craig, and I munched on sandwiches and snacks they'd brought along, and talked about traveling and cars and the past and the West and the late afternoon sun. After crossing miles of barren terrain we pulled off the freeway in Gallup, New Mexico, where Michael and Craig had planned to drop me off before they headed south. The town was desolate and had an uncanny resemblance to the area surrounding the infamous Bates Motel. There seemed little to say about it that would endear me to the local population. In a word, I felt: fucked.

I hid my anxieties and wished Michael and Craig success for the rest of their trip. They wished me well, and we exchanged warm-hearted hugs. My stomach was full, and my time had been enjoyable, but once again, this didn't seem a promising place to emerge at the same time as the desert night.

The motels were about as appealing as a Mongolian cockroach catcher's bathroom. In fact, it would probably have served my purposes better to have come across some Mongolian cockroach catchers, at least I would have been secure in having some companionship. With few cars in the parking lots, broken lights on the buildings, and no cheerful faces or signs to welcome me, I wondered if I should try to hitchhike my way out of town. I felt like I had just entered a small corner of Hell.

I apologize to all the people who actually live in Gallup,

but I can assure anyone who is thinking of moving there, it would be a monumentally bad idea. However, if you have an ex-girlfriend, -wife or -husband, it would do no harm to banish them to this sullen corner of the earth. With a sigh of real desperation, I entered the first motel I stumbled across. It was a seedy place, but as I had found out, sometimes appearances can be deceiving.

Not this time.

When I walked in, an Indian fellow came to the front desk wearing only boxer shorts; his hairy chest and belly bulging and wobbling in all fathomable directions. I had nothing to lose, so I went into my spiel about the kindness of strangers and the kind-natured American experience I had been having.

"Would you be interested in showing me some fabled American generosity?" I asked.

"I am *not* American. What do you want?" he responded, unimpressed.

"I am English . . ." Why I thought this would work I am not sure.

"So what? What do you want, don't waste my time. I was sleeping and you just woke me up!"

I could see that this was not going to go very far. "Well, it would be good karma for you . . ."

"Out!"

I politely found my way out.

And I kept moving. Two more motels, and two more rejections, both run by Indians who charged twenty to twenty-five dollars per night. Trotting to the next and last motel on the street before the road widened into a highway and the vast darkness beyond, I went inside and approached the clerk.

"Let's make a deal," I began.

Wary, he watched my hands as though fearing I would pull out a machine gun from behind my back.

"Look, I need a room just for the night. I'll leave first thing in the morning."

"You from England?" he asked.

"Yes" I answered tiredly.

"God save the Queen," he said with a smile. "I have family in England, lots of family."

"You do? Well that means we're basically brothers!" With a wide smile I reached over and grabbed him by the shoulders, and embraced him.

"Okay, you can stay, but no prostitutes or animals allowed. Understood?"

"Oh, thank you, thank you—I love you!" Jumping up and down with delight, I danced a jig of joy. I watched with unadulterated glee as he wrote out a registration form and handed me a key.

I had been saved.

I hurried out the door before my new friend could change his mind. Close to two hours after being dropped off, I was about to enter a motel room and then all I had to do was spend my two dollars on some food and I was through for the night.

Then, my world collapsed around me.

The light above the motel door was broken and only the dim yellow glow of the streetlight illuminating the sidewalk was enough for me to find my way and locate the keyhole. As I was preparing to insert the key, I noticed a strange coloration on the door and frame and mat. I swear, there was blood all over the motel room door.

I pulled back. I noticed a strange odor hung uncomfortably in the air. I could imagine returning to the motel later in the night and being murdered by some vagrant on his way to rob the resident drug dealer. I let my eyes adjust to the darkness, and stepped one stride to the left to let the streetlamp illuminate the door as best as its pathetic glow could. The bloodstains smeared across the front and side of the door were truly horrifying. There was no doubt that this was blood. Whether it was human or animal, I did not know, nor did I care to. What the hell was I going to do now?

Looking back to the dreary street, I knew my options were limited. I could either take a chance and try to find a better motel (not likely) or wander until I stumbled upon a stranger with kindness to give (again not likely). No, this was it. After some rather intense soul searching I decided to put my life in the hands of God and bunker down in the motel.

I stepped inside, with three goals: First, I would barricade myself in by moving all the furniture against the door and window to stop unwelcome intruders. Second, I would keep all my clothes on as a precaution against sudden threats which may appear. Third, and most importantly, I would pray.

None of these prepared me for the cockroaches.

As I flipped the light switch, I saw them scatter—a family of cockroaches along with their entire extended family, aunts, uncles, third cousins, and friends darted in all directions up the wall in an orgy of movement. I couldn't decide if it was more dangerous inside or outside. Once inside, I closed and locked the door. Twice. I lay on the bed for several minutes, trying to work up enough energy to take a shower. I eventually decided taking a shower was unwise, as the water was probably contaminated. I settled down in my barricaded fortress trying to wish the night away. Then the final surprise of the night erupted. I heard loud voices from the adjoining room. The night was still young for some people it seemed, although by this time it was nearly one in the morning. The voices were getting louder and more violent. I had stumbled into a family feud. Peeking through the window, I saw a large red truck and three disheveled people going in and out of their room, to the truck and back. On first glance this did not seem too bad. First glances aren't always accurate though.

"What you looking at boy?" The large hairy one yelled.

For a split second I thought he was speaking to me, but to my great relief it seemed that his wrath was directed at a younger guy, who I assumed was his son.

"At you! This is all your fault!" the son screamed.

"My fault! Are you still smoking crack, son! You ain't got no truth!" the father screamed back.

"I told you not to trust those guys. . . . You didn't listen to me."

"Why would I listen to you? You dumb fuck!"

This was all getting a little bit out of control; I had no idea what or who they were talking about, but here I was peeking out of a filthy curtain, barricaded in the planet's worst motel room, hoping that this family feud wouldn't spill over into my world. If they had seen me peeking I was history, but I was glued to this little scrap. Then, the mother chimed in.

"I've had enough of both you. You're both good for nothing drunks who should know better than to trust that bitch!"

This evidently pissed the father off.

"That's it; you are both going to pay for this." He ran

into the motel room and grabbed something and then ran to the truck.

Had it been a Hollywood movie, this was the moment when we'd hear gun shots. Luckily for me there were no gunshots, just screeching of tires as the father sped off into the darkness. I had no idea where he was going but I was hoping he would not be coming back. The son and mother ran into their room, slamming the door, and started a screaming match between themselves. The mother seemed intent on getting all her anger out and the son seemed intent on taking none of it. I made my way to the bed and the screaming match continued but I couldn't make out what they were saying. After about five minutes of ranting, silence finally descended on the motel. I triple-checked the lock and the positioning of my barricades to make sure I was fully secure from any invasion, finally falling asleep at around 3 a.m.

I woke up three hours later to quietness. I had survived the night. The moment the gray light of dawn lit the highway, I ran from the room, leaving my key on the dresser, and shaking with the memory of the bugs, the mold, the screaming . . . the blood. Reaching the highway, I waved at every passing car, and in less than an hour, I had a ride in a camper with a woman and her husband.

"You're out early!" she said cheerily. "Where'd you come from?"

I told her the name of the motel, and her face dropped. She seemed to slip into a state of shock.

"You . . . you slept there?"

"Oh my God!" said her husband.

"Oh my God!" I said back.

"The area is renowned for the . . . . darker elements of

Gallup: rapes, fights, drug deals happen all the time. So many, the news stopped covering it. Last week there was a murder at one of the motels."

I swallowed hard.

"A . . . murder?" Now it was my turn to slip into a state of shock. Surely this could not have happened in *my* motel room. This could not be possible! Or could it? I didn't want to dwell on this for too long.

I changed the subject. "So . . . I'm headed to Hollywood. What do you suggest as the fastest route?"

"Flagstaff," they said in unison, then laughed together.

"Brilliant. Flagstaff. Where do you guys live?" I asked.

"We live in Santa Barbara California."

"The home of the newly wed and the nearly dead!" said the husband, and we all chuckled together.

"But we travel a lot. Not as much as you, of course."

"Yeah, that's crazy, what you're doing."

"Is it?" I asked him. "What's the craziest thing you've ever done?"

"I don't know. Just about everything I do is crazy."

"Give me one story. That won't shock your wife."

"Craziest was probably buying this bus."

"Why?" I asked.

"I don't know, I guess it's just . . . it's just crazy owning it. Believe me, you can go crazy owning a bus. You always wonder what's going to happen next, you know."

I guess he was right there; the thought of picking up a strange Englishman was probably not on his radar when he had woken up in the morning.

The camper might have been a crazy purchase, but it was a place of total peace. After the night I'd had, I drifted off in the back, and woke only to inhale the aroma of some tacos they generously offered me. I couldn't have asked for more: a traveling oasis of calm and solitude, and a place to rest that actually got me further toward my destination.

The pair was relaxed and obviously enjoying life on the road. When we pulled into Flagstaff later that day, they asked me to come and visit them if I found my way to Santa Barbara. I decamped at a gas station and thanked them profusely, feeling lighter and happier than I could have imagined just a few hours earlier.

When people are at peace, they really are magic. Like Michael and his rusty machines that one day become shiny trophies, they can perform a resurrection. Could that happen to me? Not in one day, but in one life? Could I be alive in a way I never had been? The sense of calmness and peace I had been experiencing along the way, although amazing, was not really based in reality. The real trick was going to come when I returned to my everyday life. A life where I was going to have to utilize all the things I had learned along the way. If I was going to reshape my life, I would have to do it in the full glare of my peers, my family, and society. There would be little hope if I got back home and fell straight back into my old habits, forsaking my newly conceived plans. I had found it easier to get in touch with my courage and inner strength whilst on the road, but could I hang on to them whilst in the maelstrom of family and business life in London? Being thousands of miles away from the epicenter of my demons was a safety cushion I would not have for long.

This realization was at once sobering and disturbing. I was now completely aware that the real hard work would come when I found myself back home. How was I going to face my father and tell him I was actually leaving London to live in Los Angeles? He may have acquiesced to me leaving on this trip, but was expecting me back in the office when I finished with this youthful indiscretion. I needed to prepare myself psychologically for the trip back home and the discussions that would surely arise about my future.

I had learned a great deal about life but the real proof of my success would be in the pudding. Would I be able to find the right balance in the wider world when my journey was over? Would my family understand my desires? Would they accept me after I had explained my life changes? All I could do at that moment was play them through my mind and prepare myself for the inevitable challenges awaiting me.

But now was not the time. I had reached the center of Flagstaff, and the day's own challenges awaited.

If you ever catch on fire, try to avoid seeing yourself in the mirror, because I bet that's what really throws you into a panic.

—*Jack Handey*

In a tiny alley in the quaint city center of Flagstaff, a scrawny teenager on Rollerblades flew inches past my *head.*

The whirr of wind and sound shocked me out of my reverie of big ideas and into the present twilight of a strange city—in short, I freaked out and fell down. The little madman had jumped out from a total blind corner for some early evening stimulation and I had the misfortunate of being his victim. I lay motionless on the street and let out a few quiet, nervous yelps. Had he actually hit me, the least I would have been looking at was a trip to the emergency ward with multiple broken bones. Emerging out of my catatonic state, I yelled after him, blubbering an angry reproach.

"What the . . . what the bloody hell are you doing, man! You nearly ran me over!"

His response: a cheeky wink. The kid whose recklessness had nearly taken my life *winked* at me.

"Hey, I know the feeling."

"Huh?" I said, slowly standing up and brushing off my pants.

"Yeah, man. I got hit by a car right here."

"Well, that's not surprising," I said, picking up my backpack. But when I looked up, I was surprised. He was sticking out his hand, as if to shake.

"I'm Josh."

I looked at him for a minute. What the hell. "I'm Leon."

"Cool."

"Yeah," I said. Who was this kid? "So when did you get hit?"

"Oh, about a week ago. I broke my hip."

"Well, that seems far-fetched. You're still rollerblading."

How could he possibly still be rollerblading after suffering such an injury?

He laughed, and spun on his skates. "I dunno. I'm superman, dude," he said with a wry smile.

I couldn't help but laugh. The freedom of youth. "What other crazy shenanigans have you accomplished on your Rollerblades?" I asked.

"Oh, I'm always breaking my bones. Once I broke most of the bones in my right hand."

"How did you manage that one?"

"I crashed into a truck."

“I’ll bet your parents enjoyed receiving the phone call about that one!” I countered.

“My mom’s psychologically prepared for receiving these types of calls these days,” he said nonchalantly. “Do you want to see more of my skills?”

“Not really, but do I have a choice!”

“No.”

He was off in a flash.

“Don’t move!” he yelled over his shoulder.

Just as I was preparing to dive for the curb again, roller-boy Josh lost control and fell violently, landing on his face. I ran the thirty feet to him.

“Are you all right?” I inquired.

“Sure,” he said, ignoring my extended hand. There were no complaints and he was soon up and about continuing his death-defying stunts. With a brief “See ya!” he took off, another echo in my trek to the Coast.

“See ya,” I said to myself, and walked to the end of the alley.

One of the reactions to being so close to the Hollywood sign was that each experience was heightened—seared into my consciousness. I knew it was all soon going to be over and I wanted to take in as much of it as possible and store it for when I found myself back home. Each experience I had had along the path was going to aid me in recreating a life for myself, a life filled by inspiration. A life that would hopefully make a difference to the people I met along the way. I saw Josh, a small blurry dot in the distance, and chuckled at the ridiculous perfection of a young boy throwing caution to the wind. Wasn’t it, after all, what I was doing?

The music from the bars reached me long before I saw their neon signs. But soon, they were everywhere. I had no money for booze, but figured bars—in what seemed a friendly town—were a likely place for kindhearted souls to gather. Or so I hoped.

I popped into a particularly noisy joint just off the city square, and said hello to an older gentleman chatting up the barkeep.

"You from around here?" asked the man, a puddle of water on the bar in front of him, and an empty beer bottle beside him.

"No, I'm from England. On my way to L.A."

The server brought my new friend another beer, and I took the silence as a chance to start my story. He didn't stop me. I'd hoped to garner his interest in helping me out. It soon became clear that he was a little too interested in me.

"I live in the desert," he whispered.

"Oh," I said, ignoring the creepy tone in his voice. "Living in the desert must be somewhat of a challenge. Who do you live with?"

"No one," he said, taking a swig of his beer. "I live alone."

"Why the desert?" I probed.

"Well, it's peaceful and enables me to stay away from people." His voice was raspy and barely audible. "I don't like people so much."

Then he made me an offer. "I want you to come and stay with me tonight."

Normally, I wouldn't be picky. I needed a bed, like I always needed a bed, and normally I would have taken it from anyone. And really, I hadn't felt threatened on the trip apart from the drug dealer in downtown Indianapolis. There was the blood-stained motel room, of course, but that was more psychologically disturbing than physically endangering. But this chap was different. I was low on sleep and food and there was nothing casual about this guy's voice or eye movements. I felt like I was being propositioned by the local serial killer.

My options? Wander bars and streets and search for shelter, or . . . head off into the middle of the desert with a stranger who seemed devoid of real social skills and spoke in whispers.

Perhaps I could let him down gently. . . .

"When are you going back home?" I asked.

"I normally leave for home when I have found someone . . ."

That's it. Decision made.

"I have to go and get supplies, but afterwards we can make our way to my cabin. When I have guests over, which isn't often, I make a fire and we sit around and chat all night. Then you sleep."

"Then *I* sleep? What, uh, may I ask, do you do?" What the fuck? This was turning into a possible nightmarish scenario.

He just smiled.

"Well," I said, standing up. "Thanks for your offer of a bed tonight, but I think I am going to stay around town," I told him.

"All right, you lose," he said, paying his tab and getting up to leave. "Good night."

"Good night," I managed, and collapsed on the bar in relief when the door closed behind him.

My trip was about trust, kindness, interdependence. But the fact remains: humanity's not perfect. As a whole, I believe we are full of more good than evil, more light than dark, and my journey was nothing if not total confirmation of humanity's innate goodness, of the benefit we all bring to one another if we're open to it. But in our search—and certainly in my search—for connection, we have to be alert. We all have a sixth sense built into us: we feel people out.

People are always sizing each other up and then making decisions based on these initial internal sign posts. We have to. The challenge? To make these assessments in the context of openness. It's too easy—too lazy a response—to close the door on everyone right away. We have to learn to trust ourselves. And I was beginning to.

I walked out of the bar consumed by the very real pressure of finding a room. I headed into a partially hidden alleyway lined with restaurants. I stumbled across a burrito place a few doors down and attempted to find someone who could give me a place to stay; no one was having any of my British charm. I then changed my tact and pleaded for food. No luck. I noticed two girls chatting in a corner booth, and I waved casually. They waved me over.

"Hello, ladies!"

"Hello. You don't look like a homeless guy . . ."

"Oh, I'm not! I have a home—a nice one! I'm just in the middle of an experiment and the success of it depends on my not having a home for a little while."

They looked at me curiously.

"Okay, I'm stumbling because you're pretty. But if you give me sixty seconds, I'll tell you a great story that explains it all."

They looked at each other and laughed. The blonde girl reached for her wrists and fiddled with her watch.

"Okay," she said. "Sixty seconds. . . . Go!"

And I went. My story in a minute, and, in my opinion, it was pretty good. At one point, I dove on the floor; at another, I leapt in the air. If I'd been begging, it would have at least been worth a dollar bill.

"Wow," said the brown-haired girl with green eyes. "Touch the Hollywood sign, huh? Think you'll make it?"

"I do. But there's always a chance I'll fail. Every day I have to find a stranger willing to help. And right now, the day is dying and the street is looking more and more like my bed for the evening."

"Can't let that happen, can we, Joy?"

"No," said the apparently-named Joy. "No we cannot."

To add icing on the cake, when the manager of the burrito place saw I had found people willing to take a risk on me, she gave me a whole burrito free.

"Flagstaff," I said to myself, "is no Gallup."

"Gallup? Are you kidding? You went there?"

"I am not kidding, though I wish I were."

"Well, I guarantee our place is better than any motel in Gallup."

I just smiled. "Girls, so long as there is no blood on the door, your guarantee shall be fulfilled."

"You talk funny. Doesn't he, Haley?"

"A little, but I like it. I don't know anyone who says the word *shall!*"

We walked to their apartment. One of Joy and Haley's friends was waiting on their porch. As we sat there, enjoying the crisp evening air, we started swapping stories. His by far, was the most fantastic I had heard so far. (Well, fantastic may not be the right word if you are a parent sending your kids to an Arizona summer camp.)

Richard was a camp counselor and he told me his story

with a caveat that I not repeat it to anyone—but I just can't help myself. (Sorry, Richard.)

One summer, Richard had ten young boys in his charge. They had set off on a wilderness hike, a journey to manhood—or to elevenhood—following their compasses and the stars. "The aim of the trip was to teach them about nature and, you know, its role in society. How nature and society meet," he explained.

"So one of the first lessons was going to be how *not* to light a fire in the wilderness. You know how to do it wrong. We teach them this, so they know how to do it right."

This is not how we teach children in Britain, but Americans have taken over the world, so I sat silently and nodded. Perhaps there is some hidden genius in this reverse instruction.

As it turns out, the one way *not* to light a fire is to pour gasoline all over an existing fire. Wind, they say, may cause blowback and engulf the person pouring the gasoline. Generally, it is understood by many that this is the thing that must *never* be done. Richard, in his earnest desire to teach the kids what not to do, picked up the container of gasoline and poured it atop a raging fire.

"You know, to demonstrate why this wasn't a good idea," he said.

"Of course," I replied, nodding.

Sure enough, a gust of wind blew the gasoline onto a nearby ten-year-old, who was immediately engulfed in flames.

"I mean, my career stood in the balance!" Richard said excitedly, remembering the scene.

"As did the life of a small child," I gently reminded him.

"Oh, yes! Of course! That too!"

The boy was saved when the other boys began doing the most natural thing a boy does: they threw mud and sand upon him, while others shoved him to the ground and jumped on him. Despite a few minor burns, the kid was fine. The rest of the crew got to throw dirt and beat up a fellow member. And everyone learned how not to start a fire.

All in all, a good day.

It's a shame I can't mention names of people or names of camps. Sorry, Arizona parents. And good luck.

To add another twist to the story, when the incident was reported, Richard was saved from the wrath of the "wilderness" police when the boy engulfed in flames took the blame for the mishap.

I tried to get reassurances from Richard, that he was not planning on setting me on fire. He assured me he wasn't.

I was given the couch for the night, and hoped Richard would soon go home. Waking up on fire was not in my plans.

The next day came early and bright. Haley dropped me off in the town center to seek my way further west. With my daily five dollars, I splurged on breakfast and spent all my money in one fell swoop. I was fully broke by 9:30 a.m.

As I found my way to a gas station by the freeway, I spotted a road sign. It read:

Los Angeles: 450 miles.

In a flash, my whole trip came into sharp perspective. I had put 2,500 miles behind me. My odyssey was eyeing its own conclusion. The Hollywood sign was less than half a day in a fast classic car, or a family trailer, or the bouncy cap of a big heavy truck. I was *close*—so close I could taste the sea breeze on the coast of California. The horizon was coming into focus. A surge of pride moved within me, for the man who would stand before the sign was a different person from the man who had conceived the idea on his couch in London. The trip had never really been about reaching Hollywood. Los Angeles wasn't even really a place to me, only an idea. It was about what I could do to help others in return for the aid they had given me: how we could give and receive on a human level, soul to soul, story to story. It was about learning who I was or wanted to become.

Tears welled up in my eyes as I realized the implications of reaching the end. I had started the trip as a confused boy; and I was on the cusp of becoming a man. I had weathered many a storm and my final calling was about to become reality. I felt the urge to shed my old skin and reclaim a life I felt had been half-lived. My transformation from boy to man was being played out in front of my eyes. I was finding my way through the murkiness of life with the help of people I met on the path.

Los Angeles. Ten letters. Two words. Not even English originally. The longer I looked at it, the less it became a verbal entity. The white letters, against that familiar green metal on the highways of America, separated, and became foreign symbols. It might as well have been a painting or a blurry photograph or a beautiful foreign script—a pure symbol separated from meaning on its own, and simply a thing of beauty. It was validation that everything had actually been worth it. It was validation that my trek meant something. It was my life I was improving. It was my life

I had been wasting. Through the interconnectedness of humanity I had been lifted to reach for the stars.

By this time, tears were streaming down my face. The moment had gotten the better of me. My life flashed before my eyes as I sat there in the scorching heat of an Arizona morning. I allowed the tears to flow, realizing the internal pressure of my previous life was finally getting the chance to speak. Tears came, and more after them.

I had reached *the* turning point. A point where it became crystal clear to me that there was no turning back. My future did not lie in the family business, or the stultified world of corporate finance. My future was in the arts. My future was in the rarified world of writing. My future was in Los Angeles. My future was in reclaiming the lost soul that had floundered for so many years. My future was in giving back to people. My future was in *giving* whatever gifts I had acquired through this trip.

My future.

Not someone else's perception of my future. I felt a freedom. I felt a lightness. I felt free. My trip, although not over, was bringing its gifts to my world. My future was now. All I had to do was complete the journey. I wiped away the tears, and turned back to the station.

And saw the ugliest dog I'd ever seen.

"Come on, Mooch," an elderly man said, emerging from the store and calling after the dog. His tail was wagging furiously, though he hobbled as badly as his owner. Mooch, I'd later learn, was eighteen years old. His owner, the elderly Ed, had seen him born, had hunted with him, walked with him, ridden with him, for nearly two decades. For a couple of hours, Ed let me ride with his best friend, and Mooch seemed okay with sharing the front seat for a few miles. He rested his head in my lap, and looked as tired and happy as I was. By the time we reached Kingman, I felt Mooch a good friend, and Ed a man at peace with age and life, with the past and the future. After all, he'd found his companion for all these many years. I said good-bye to them both in the parking lot of a Kmart, and tossed my bag on my back. The world was spinning as it always had; Ed was with Mooch as he'd always been; and I was on the road, as I was meant to be. The end was nigh.

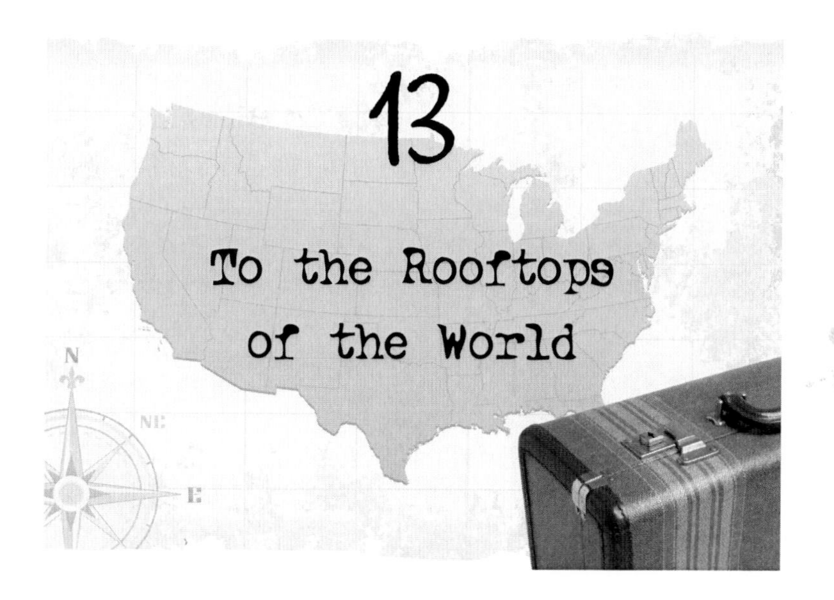

13

To the Rooftops of the World

There is only one success—to be able
to spend your life in your own way.

—*Christopher Morley*

I've never considered the big box stores of America very attractive. The Wal-Marts and Best Buys and Home Depots. Driving and training and walking across the U.S., I'd seen them everywhere, in small town and urban centers, sitting lonely on large highways and crammed between skyscrapers. Not once did I find them appealing. Efficient perhaps, and well-stocked, but never inviting or personal.

But when Ed and Mooch dropped me at the Kmart in Kingman just as the sun was descending over the top of the big box retailer, just as the warm blacktop of the parking lot was beginning to cool, just as the evening work crew was arriving and slipping in the side door, there was something simple and beautiful about the scene. Maybe I was still high from my realization that Los Angeles was within reach, or maybe I was beginning to settle into a new way of seeing the world.

Kingman was unquestionably the smallest town I had been in so far—which was saying a lot. I saw no houses, only lots of trees and open land, and began to wonder if the rural flavor would work in my favor (friendly country people!) or against me (skeptical country people). Turns out, I wouldn't even have to find out.

From behind me roared a Kingman municipal fire truck. It pulled up right next to me, and a large, overalled man popped out and chirped a good evening. It was as if the universe were aligning itself, and sending me people who were not only inclined to help me, but obligated to do so. (Taxpayer dollars, and all that.)

"Good evening!" I offered, following him into Kmart, as his comrade waved from the cab. "I wonder if you'd be willing to put an Englishman up for the night?"

He looked back at the cab and gave his colleague a look. "We, uh, we don't do charity."

I glanced back at his partner, who was now leaning partly out the window, with what seemed to be a mix of both curiosity and compassion.

"Well, let's not look at it as charity. I like to call it kindness, and it's gotten me from Times Square in New York to this very spot."

They looked at each other again. "Well, Randy?" the big one asked the man in the cab, who shrugged in agreement. "Okay, let's call the Captain."

If I was going to be allowed to stay the night it had to be approved by the head man (there was a head honcho in every situation in America, always someone higher up the chain to ask). He whipped out a heavy cell phone and punched in a number.

"Hey, Cap. I got a guy here, an English guy, who needs a place for the night. Thought you could talk to him."

"Put him on!" the phone squawked.

"Here you go," said the fireman. "Be impressive."

"Hello, sir. Captain, sir."

"What do you need?"

"I really need a place to stay tonight."

"Are you joking around with me?" he responded curtly.

"No, no. I actually am very bad at jokes. I really do need your help."

"Where are you from?"

"London."

"How do I know you are genuine and not some vagabond spinning a story?"

I actually laughed. "I have so many stories to recount that only a madman could actually make these up. Let me come over, and I'll tell you all about it. I'm traveling from one end of America to the other, and you've got a chance to give firefighters everywhere a really good name!"

He paused. "All right then, come on over." His tone was unconvinced.

I did a small twirl in front of the firefighter before handing him the phone back. He looked at me strangely.

"Oh, sorry."

"Yeah. Don't do that when we get to the station."

Fifteen minutes later, I found myself at the gates of the station, and was welcomed by a friendly, if somewhat physically imposing, bunch of guys, who kept asking me to say things in my British accent, while laughing and slapping me on the back so frequently I felt bruised and shaken up—but welcomed. When the Captain arrived, he asked me to keep my promise.

"Leon, I need some stories. Prove you're not a madman. Give us details."

"Yessir!" I saluted to awkward silence. "Sorry. Just kidding."

I threw myself into the tales, recounting some of my most fantastical stories, I told them of Cinnamon and my escapades with the Indianapolis drug dealer. I mentioned the wrestling priest and Gene the astronaut and his wife, the maker of too many cookies. I told them about Rick and his separated shoulder, no health insurance, and illiteracy. And I told them about Julie, who gave me her keys and house without a second thought. And I told them about the blood-stained door in Gallup. I did not tell them about Katherine. I wasn't yet ready to talk about her to anyone but myself. She was, it seemed, my secret inspiration.

"Well, ain't that a helluva thing," said the Captain when I was finished.

"It certainly is."

"I'll tell you, Leon, we're a family here. Brothers. And we take care of each other. Seems you know a little bit about that. And far be it from us to give up a chance to be part of one helluva good story." He looked at the guys, all of them in blue pants and overalls. "Boys, what do you say? Should we give ole Leon a bed for the night?"

It was unanimous. More back-slapping ensued, and my evening plans were set.

The camaraderie the firemen possessed was evident, and just as it had nourished me across the country, I could see how it was nourishing them as well. I could hardly now remember a time when I didn't know how to make that connection, when I didn't think it was even a real possibility. That part of my life was fast receding into the recesses of the past. Here I was in the middle of nowhere tasting the camaraderie with these welcoming strangers. I felt this was a major reason why firemen sacrificed the way they did. It was a sense of helping the common good and also the very real sense of interconnectedness.

Randy came over to me and pointed to the corner. "There's your room. Make yourself comfortable. . . . Oh," he said, turning back for a second. "I left a little present in there for you." He grinned and closed the door.

I wandered to the side room and found the space they'd kindly given me for that night. A small bed in one corner, a single locker next to it, and stuck on the wall with a push-pin, what I could only guess was Randy's "gift": a calendar featuring pictures of—you guessed it—firemen, their faces marked with markers. I supposed this was the equivalent of an office joke.

Asleep in a few minutes, the next sound I heard was a knock on the door, and the curious, compassionate Randy from the day before asking me if I wanted some coffee and biscuits.

"Oh, and you can take that calendar with you if you want," he laughed. "You know, as a souvenir." I snatched it off the wall and crammed it in my bag.

"Let me guess: Las Vegas?"

"You got it! Headed there?"

"Buddy, everybody here is headed to Vegas. No place else to go!"

I hopped in the cab of Larry's R.V. and we hit the road out of Kingman. The guys at the firehouse had told me to just stick my hand in the air on the westbound highway and I'd get a ride in no time. This was illegal, of course, they warned me, but it was Kingman, and half the people hitched to work and home.

"It's a friendly kind of place," they had said. And they were right.

"Plenty of traffic bound for Sin City," Larry said. "It's where everybody takes their wallets and wishbones for the weekend."

"You ever won big?"

"Me?" Larry laughed. "No, no. I don't gamble. I go for the easy payout: the buffets!"

Oh, the buffets. Of course. This was America, the land of plenty, and of plenty more than you need. Which reminded me: I was starving, and there was a bag of chips between us I couldn't stop staring at.

"Stare at those any harder and you're gonna burn 'em up! Take a few if you want."

"Larry, you are a kind and gentle soul."

He laughed. But he was, and turned out to be on a spiritual quest of his own. His father had recently died and he was roaming the country in search of some reflection and inner peace.

"How is it going, if you don't mind my asking?"

He was silent for a moment. "I think the going is what's important. Sitting in my house, I just kept thinking he'd walk in, or he'd call. Out here, I don't expect to see him or hear him. Maybe I'll get used to that."

I had no reply. My father was a world away, not just in miles, but in mind. How far he had traveled from his father's world, and how far I had come from his. We were very different people, my father and I. So different I wondered what, if anything, we had in common. My trip was not about my father, like Larry's. At least not concretely. But in some ways, it was. My departure from my old life was partly about leaving behind the expectations he had for me, and the shadow he cast that I had for so long lived beneath. But sitting there with Larry, I wondered if, once that shadow was gone, if I wouldn't long for its cool shade.

The trip was peaceful, and it was now my turn to listen. Larry recounted how the loss of his father had deeply affected him: "It tore out a part of my soul," he said. "I need some time to put my house back in order."

"I hope you do, Larry."

Soon, the Welcome to Las Vegas sign screamed its welcome to *us*, and in a heartbeat we were sucked into the strip. I said my good-byes to Larry at the legendary Mirage Hotel, where he was "heading to the trough," and I was off to see America's playground.

Vegas does things to you. The moment you're in the vortex, you begin to think differently. The flashing lights and pounding music envelope you, and the real world seems to melt away. It's like a virtual reality game: you know your body is still in the real world, but your mind is captured by the machine. I wandered into one of the hundred casinos, and walked around the slots and contemplated changing all my five dollars so I could play the penny slots.

It dawned on me that of all the rules I'd placed on myself for the journey, I had not ruled out gambling as a possible source of income. Why had I not thought of this before?! I could play and win! I could become rich! I could show up at the Hollywood sign already a millionaire!

I changed my five-dollar bill and sat down in front of a blinking machine. A coin, a pull of the lever, a musical sound, a loss. Again. Again. Loss. Loss. Loss. One by one, my coins dwindled. In less than ten minutes, I was broke.

This was why I had not thought of gambling before. It was not the best idea.

I reached into my pocket searching for one final coin, and my finger brushed Katherine's tiny toy coyote. The slight touch brought me back to my senses. I laughed at myself and my delusions, took a last look at the dozens of middle-aged Americans pulling the slot levers, and walked out onto the strip.

My mission, the usual: a place to stay, a meal, and a ride across the last spot of desert to the promised land of Los Angeles.

I went from hotel to hotel repeatedly facing the bitter taste of rejection. One hotel manager threatened to arrest me for loitering. I was going to have to get wilier when it came to finding a place to stay. Sitting down on the curb outside the casino in the blazing heat, I thought how like the gambling mecca of Las Vegas my trip had become. I had invested everything: my health, time, and energy, to discover my true path. There had been epic wins and losses along the way.

A roll of the dice and you could win it all.

I'd never considered myself a gambler. The ten minutes in the casino were the only minutes I'd ever spent gambling. But as I sat, baking in the desert sun, I felt that maybe I was more of a gambler than I'd thought. I had taken a huge risk by leaving the comfort of my home, a gamble which had definitely paid off. If I had remained at home I would still be continuing down the well-trodden path of mediocrity.

Instead, I had gambled it all. I took a life less lived and risked it all on a crapshoot across America. I might be losing in Vegas but I was winning the bigger game.

Vegas may be pretty, in a fabricated, inauthentic way, but I know bad things must happen there. Prostitution. Illegal gambling. Drugs and alcohol in unhealthy doses. Various other unspeakable acts. In such an environment, aptly named Sin City, and not ironically, one would think the police force would be occupied protecting and serving the visitors and citizens of such a lively and electric city against the drug lords, the mobsters, the sex traffickers, and, of course, the jaywalkers.

I bounded across the street, energized and ready to roll the dice once more on a human connection. I reached the other side only to be accosted by a policeman on a bike, who slid dramatically to stop next to me.

"Excuse me, sir! Do you know the light was red?" he asked abruptly.

I was taken aback. "Uh, no, I didn't."

"Well, it was, and you crossed anyway. That's illegal."

"Oh, sorry, I'll make sure next time I stop at the light," I said, and I started to walk off. This was my first mistake.

"Sir, where do you think you are going? Stay here or you are going to have some serious problems."

"Are you being serious?" I laughed.

This was my second mistake.

He put his face right up to mine and grabbed my arm, dragging me toward the curb to highlight his level of seriousness. (Dragged would only be a minor exaggeration.)

"If you don't cooperate with me I will take you to the station and file charges against you for jaywalking!"

"Um, jaywalking? Are you being bloody serious? This is complete lunacy. Don't you have anything better to do than stop people for jaywalking?"

This was my third, and nearly fatal, mistake.

He fixed an icy stare on me. "I advise you to stop talking back to me. Jaywalking is illegal and now you are going to get a citation. You're not in England anymore!"

I finally caught on that the best way out of the situation was to keep my mouth shut. To add injury to my already deflated ego, I felt humiliated as people walked by giving me telling stares.

He wrote furiously on his little pad and tore off the ticket with a flourish. "Here," he said, pushing it into my chest. "Be sure to answer within forty-five days. You can pay by check or credit card."

"Pay? Pay what exactly?"

"The citation fee for jaywalking, mister: $180."

"A hundred and eighty dollars?! Are you—"

The icy stare again.

I remained silent, and watched him get back on his bike and pedal off to save the city from other criminals, like meter violators and gum chewers.

I spun away angrily, and lost my balance in the process slipping to the sidewalk in a lump. The sun was hot, but I seemed to be sweating more than I should. I looked at my hands, which were now trembling. Was I that angry? Over a stupid ticket?

"Young man, you okay?"

I looked up to see a short man in a bright red T-shirt approaching me.

"Had a bit of a collision with the local police?"

"Jaywalking . . . $180 . . . jaywalking . . ." I seemed unable to form a coherent sentence.

"Forgive me, young man, but you don't look too well." He touched me on the shoulder, lightly.

"I—I don't, don't, feel . . . no, I do not." The corners of my vision were turning dark, and what was left of the light was blurring fast. Soon, the earth was spinning.

"Young man?" His lips were moving, and he stood not a few inches from me, but the sound was distant, bouncing in a canyon far away. I saw him motion quickly, his arms moving in a blur of red. I felt myself leaning backward, and in a moment, I was flat on the sidewalk.

"Leon!" A familiar voice. "Leon! Leon, stay with us, buddy." It was Nick, Mr. Invisible, the man offstage filming my antics for posterity, now emerging as I drifted toward unconsciousness.

"Leon, buddy, did you eat today? Anything? Leon, look at me—have you had anything? Your blood sugar, remember?"

Of course I remembered. It had been on my mind every day, every morning and afternoon, knowing the results of my tests, knowing that with every day I was on the road, without proper meals or proper beds, my health, or what was left of it, was deteriorating.

"This is not good. Okay, sir. SIR!" Nick was talking intently to the man with the red T-shirt. "Sir, I need you to run over there and grab my satchel, okay? It has my cell phone, and I need it right now."

The older gentleman scurried across the street, without any concern for possibly watching policemen, and grabbed the bag, while Nick slid my backpack off my back and placed it under my head. A small crowd had gathered, pausing to watch the sick Englishman before hitting the blackjack tables. I was, I suppose, delaying their losses for a few minutes. This was a small consolation.

Nick grabbed the satchel from my well-dressed friend, and whipped out his cell phone.

"What are you doing?" I mumbled.

"Calling 911! . . . Hello?" They'd picked up. "Yes, hi, my friend is sick, and—what?—I don't know. Sir, where are we?"

"You're outside the Mirage Hotel, by the entrance with the white lions . . . and . . . and there's an ambulance across the street." Everyone looked up in unison, and sure enough, an ambulance was swinging through traffic directly toward us. Nick hung up, and stood to greet an emergency officer who was jogging toward the scene, to me a blue blur with a squawking radio. I could hear Nick speaking to the guy, as another E.M.T. joined them. My head was hurting badly; I couldn't keep my eyes open. The last thing I remember was whispering to Nick to ask them if I could maybe have a bed in the hospital for free.

"At death's door," he grinned, "and you're still the biggest mooch."

Fifteen minutes later, I was sitting in the back of the ambulance with a needle in my arm, an orange juice in my hand, and a large bag of oddly colored fluid dripping into my body. The crowd had dispersed, and now only a kind uniformed lady was reading the gauge on the blood pressure machine they had encircling my arm. The ambulance's lights were no longer flashing, and I was beginning to remember what it felt like to not want to rip my own head off due to the pain. I had evidently fainted and felt a pounding pain in my head, though things were now clearer as I was being nursed back to immediate health. However, I still felt weak, felt like I could have slept for days. Certainly part of this was that I had just suffered a near-miss with my borderline diabetes. And part of it was the trip; with the end so close, my body was saying it was ready to quit.

"Just a little while longer," I mumbled softly to myself.

"What's that?" asked the attendant.

"Oh, nothing," I answered. I was simply too tired to tell my story.

Nick stood ten or fifteen meters away, talking on his cell phone, casting worried glances over his shoulder at me every now and then. He turned and began to walk toward me. I managed a smile. He looked grim.

"How you feeling? Up for a chat?"

"With whom?"

He reached out the open phone, and I took it, looking at him, puzzled.

"Hallo?" I scratched.

"Leon?"

"Dad?"

"Leon, are you all right?"

I couldn't speak for a moment. These were not the circumstances under which I wanted to speak to him. I should be talking to him from the top of the H on the Hollywood sign, not sitting weak and wounded in the back of this damn ambulance.

"Leon?"

"I'm here, Dad, and I'm fine."

"You neither sound fine, nor have friends who will lie for you. Nick has told us that you are as ill as your mother feared you'd be. She called you and told you—"

"Dad, I know, I know."

"Good, good. Then I've instructed Nick to get you to a hotel there."

"Dad—"

"—and then tomorrow, Nick will get you on a plane for home. I've given him my credit card information, and you'll fly home and we'll have an appointment set up with my physician for the day after, and . . ."

My head was swimming once more, but not for lack of sugar or lack of water or sleep. The world had formed a circle, and it was closing in on me, here, one stretch of highway away from Los Angeles. My life circle was threatening to loop around, and all I could hear above my father's pronouncements was the raspy voice of my gym teacher: "Logothetis . . . never amount to anything . . . always relying on his father . . ."

"—Leon, we'll get you home. Now that you've had your little adventure—"

"Dad—"

"Look, it was a risk, and I can admire that, but there's a fine line between risk and stupidity—"

"Dad, stop. I'm not coming back."

"That's not an option, Leon. This is . . . this is not going to work, son. You're sick and you've known it, you've worried your mother sick, too, she can't even come to the phone, and—"

"Dad, this isn't about her, or you. It's about me. And what I have to do." My voice was louder now, the attendant slinked away, and Nick had stepped back a few feet.

"Leon—"

"Do you remember the sea cave, Dad?

"Son, what does that have to do—"

"The sea cave, Dad. Just . . . do you remember?"

He paused. "Around the cape, in Greece, near your grandmother's house?"

"I never swam to it. Could never do it. Never trusted that if I went with you, I'd make it back."

"Well you were never a very good swimmer, Leon."

"But I was! I was a good swimmer! I just never believed I could swim that far, and you never believed it either. You never thought I could do it, so you never pushed me to."

He was silent.

"Dad?"

He sighed. "Yes."

"This is the sea cave. And I'm almost out the other side. And I made it because of all the people I met and these incredible, crazy people who gave me air and life and . . . Dad, I have to do this."

Again he was silent.

"I'm hanging up now, Dad. Tell Mom I love her. I'll call you when I'm finished."

Silence.

"Bye, Dad."

"Leon . . ."

I paused.

"I knew you could swim it. I did. I just . . ." I heard a heavy exhale over the line, and several moments of silence. "You ring us when you surface, won't you?"

I sighed a small smile. "When I surface."

I clicked the phone closed and sat heavily. Nick turned back to me. "Leon . . ."

"Don't."

"Leon, how are you going to finish? You can't hitch. We can't let you wander without food or shelter for who knows how many hours while you hope for help. This is not day one or three or ten, Leon. You have nothing left. Your body has nothing left."

I shook my head. I would not hear it.

"Leon, listen. It's already been a success. You've already—"

"Nick, stop. This is *not* the end. How can this be the end? It's Las Vegas! You can't end a life-changing pilgrimage in Vegas!" I smiled. He grinned slightly. "You're a good friend, Nick. But you can't stop me here."

"God, I know that. Why do you think I recruited your father to try to talk you out of it!"

I smiled at him. It was a good try.

"So if I can't stop you, then, let me help."

He put his arm on my shoulder, and looked over his at his car, the one he'd driven cross country, following wherever I'd gone, watching the journey unfold like a ghost watches the world go by. Then he looked back at me.

"Last leg," he said. "What do you say we do it together."

I was startled for a moment, and a bit confused. After a moment, we both started laughing, and began to laugh harder and harder. The E.M.T. was confused, and the attendant looked at me oddly. I tried to gain my composure. Here was the magic of revelation. Before me stood Nick, my friend, who had said he'd come along, stay at a distance, and capture what he could on camera. Nick, who had actually encouraged me to take the trip. He had been the consummate producer this day, taking charge, handling the crisis. For the first time, as I looked at him from my seat on the stretcher inside the ambulance, I realized that he was, in fact, a walking, talking, real life example of what I'd been searching for. This journey was about kindness and strangers and the goodness of the human community, but it was also just about me, a guy who wanted to learn how to connect with another human being, how to rely, to trust, to love, and *accept* love.

After these weeks of relying on strangers, here, at my perhaps most dangerous moment, the perfect conclusion of my journey revealed itself. After so much kindness from strangers, in the end I would be saved by the kindness of a friend. My heart warmed a bit, and I felt what I'd failed to feel for so many years: connected.

"Well," I smiled, wiped my eyes from the laughter's tears, and said what I'd said so many times this trip. "Have time for a story?"

Nick smiled back, and reached into the ambulance for my backpack. "Why don't you tell me while we are en route?"

"En route where?"

He removed his glasses and wiped a bit of dust from the lens. "To the City of Angels, of course."

I drifted off somewhere along the desert drive, while Nick and I were talking, recounting the entire journey, bit by bit, story by story, face by face. It seemed fitting that now, as the lights of L.A. cast their magic glow into the evening sky, we were approaching the end of the road together, that having discovered connection across the country, I would discover the meaning of true friendship here at the end, and that friend would be my escort to the most western of continental American states and the land I'd sought for weeks. We pulled over in a small parking lot near the sea.

"One last adventure?" I said, a glimmer in my eye.

"You up to it?" he asked, concern on his face.

"Let's go out in style!" I said, and opened the car door into the breeze coming off the water. I walked to the beach in Venice, the stars surprisingly bright despite the glow of the big city's fake light. The boardwalk was surprisingly busy at such a late hour, with young people half-clothed and laughing in groups on the sand.

I could barely contain myself. I didn't care that it was past midnight or that I was miles from the Hollywood sign. I knew it was close and I wanted to run there immediately. My legs were weary. Despite my sense of urgency, the Hollywood sign would have to wait one more night.

Where there's youth, there's hostels, and hostels I could handle. Couldn't be worse than Philly, and certainly not worse than Gallup. I wandered in and out of the many hostels dotted around the darkness of Venice. I asked at the first and met rejection. The second was the same. The third was similar, if a bit more hostile, and the fourth was locked and no one responded to my knocking. I was tired, but undaunted. At this point, so close to my destination, and with so many memories of kindness to support me, my confidence was high. It would, as it always had, work out in the end.

How could it not?

I climbed the stairs of the last hostel on the strip, where the night clerk looked at me with unadulterated suspicion.

I was done with the games. "Hi. I'm Leon. From the U.K. Can I stay here tonight please?"

"Do you have any money?"

"Nope."

"I'm not the owner; and consequently I don't have the authority to let you stay for free without his permission," Matt said. "You can talk to him if you want."

"I'll do that."

"Okay. But. You should know it won't do you any good."

"I've heard that before," I mumbled.

Matt led me to the owner's office and introduced us.

"Take a seat," the man with a bushy beard said. "What's going on?"

"In less than twenty-four hours, I will have completed what my father said was impossible, what my family thought was ridiculous, what most of my acquaintances, new and old, thought was useless and a waste of time. I will have traveled across the United States with nothing on me, and no resources, relying solely on the kindness of strangers. And tomorrow, when I touch the Hollywood sign, I'll have achieved a major transition—"

"You can't touch the Hollywood sign."

"I've been told I couldn't make this journey happen, but I have, and I'm so close now, I don't see why I won't—"

"No, no. I mean, you can't actually touch the sign. It's illegal."

I took a step back. "You mean, I can't, actually, touch it?"

"Nope. There are gates and cameras, and you can't do it. Sorry."

What did this mean? Obviously the sign was a symbol more than anything else. So what if I couldn't touch it, right? But hearing that it was off limits somehow deflated me. Suddenly I was too tired to stand, and I slumped down into a nearby chair.

The bearded man looked at his young worker, and then back at me.

"You okay?"

"Yeah, just . . . disappointed, I guess."

"Well, it sounds like you've already done what you wanted to do. You made it here, to California, to L.A. And you did it with the help of those you met. Wasn't that the point?"

I looked up at him. "It was the point, yes. Yes. And I did it, didn't I?"

"You did. But tonight, you have to sleep. And perhaps I can help. But, tell me, Leon. Why should I help you? You seem like a genuine guy, but there are so many people out there like you. What makes you so special, that I should go out of my way to help?"

It was here that it all truly clicked.

If I lived my life concentrating all my energies on myself I was doomed. It was about sharing with people my progress as a man. It was about showing people that living a great life is about giving back to others. It's about finding your true passions and then utilizing those passions to create meaningful change in the wider world. If this chap didn't help, so be it, I was still going to be able to find my way to a better life when all this was over.

I was free.

"I'm not in it for me. I mean, I am. I was. But I'm really in it for you. And for him. And for everybody else. I'm doing this to inspire others, to prove that we are better than we think."

He looked at me softly. "What can you give back to people if I help you? You are leaving us tomorrow, correct?"

"What would you like me to do?" I asked.

Astonishingly, what this man wanted *was* for me to give back to others in my life. He wanted me to take this experience and make a difference in people's lives. He wanted me to live the best life I could possibly imagine in order to show others that we can all go out and live a life filled with worth. One doesn't need to have special powers or fame to make a difference. Sometimes making a difference starts in the most unexpected places. Here I was in a nondescript youth hostel in Venice philosophizing with a complete stranger urging me to go out with a bang.

"I want you to be a man of your word and inspire others to create the life of their dreams. Can you do that?"

I nodded, for some reason eager to please him, eager to keep the promise. "I can."

"There's no check-up system, you know. I can't ever find out if you have."

"That's the point, isn't it?"

He smiled. "Matt, give Leon some keys, would you? I don't think he will cause us any problems tonight."

"Thanks . . ."

"Victor."

"That's a great name."

"I like it. But you can't have it. It's mine." He smiled and turned back to his desk.

"How far, do you think?"

Matt looked at the computer. "Well, it says about ten miles."

"Hmmm. That's quite a ways. Maybe I could hitch?"

"In L.A.? Not likely. Oh! I know! Use the bike!"

"You have a bike?"

"Well, I don't, but there's this old one behind the hostel. Been there forever. You could use it."

I could hardly contain myself. If this was true and the bike was actually in good working order, I would get to the Hollywood sign under my own steam.

When I saw the bike my heart sank. It was practically falling apart. There was no way this antique was going to get me very far.

"It's a piece of shit, isn't it?" Matt said.

"This isn't going to work."

"Oh ye of little faith," came Matt's reply. He wrestled it out of the weeds and set it on the sidewalk and pushed it forward, running along beside it. "See? No problem. A little air in those tires and you'll be fine!"

Off I went, waving good-bye to Matt the way I used to wave good-bye to my mother when I'd head to school on my own bicycle. The morning was cool and clear, and the breeze in my face was as perfect as the wind off the Aegean Sea in Greece. I was moving fast, map in hand, headed to the Hollywood hills.

Three miles in: the first sign of trouble.

Something snapped loudly, and I was forced to the curb. I laid the bike on its side and found the front brakes in a tangled mess. I was left with only the rear brakes, but it was certainly still usable. Puffing and panting uphill, steering carefully downhill, I plugged away. By noon, my legs were a cause for concern. I pulled over to rest under the shade of a palm tree. I was sweating badly, and growing dehydrated quickly. To make matters worse, an old soccer injury was flaring up and I was unable to put any real pressure on my left thigh. This meant the majority of the trip would have to be completed under the power of my right leg to pedal, and my left hand to brake.

Pedaling uphill from the shoreline past Santa Monica's

business district and shops, I saw the famous sign beckoning me to Beverly Hills, the playground of the rich and famous. The houses were oversized, the shrubbery perfect, the sidewalks clean and straight.

Aching with every push of the pedals, I drove the bike up one impossibly steep street after another. The roads wound together, bending this way and that, snaking their way up the Hollywood hills. The bike was useless at this point, and I could likely walk better than I was riding. Finally, when I just wanted to get off and throw it down the hill, I crested a small rise and caught my first glimpse of the sign. The large block letters standing like sentinels overlooking the city they described. I couldn't believe how beautiful it was.

Jumping off the seat, I pushed my legs up the slope. I was limping and sweating and bent over ungracefully at the waist as I plodded slowly up the dusty hill. I pushed myself, one foot in front of the other, pausing to catch my breath more than once. Finally, grabbing a clump of brush to pull myself upward one last time, I emerged directly beside the sign. No more than thirty yards from its base.

There were security cameras overlooking it, and the steep hill dared me to try to climb it. The massive letters stood silent and still, as though they'd been waiting for me. I collapsed in the grass and stared at them for a moment before turning my gaze toward the city below, the great horizontal metropolis that spread thinly over the miles and miles below. I was literally, at this moment, on top of the world.

I stood, wobbly on tired legs, thrust my hands in the air, and said thank you to the friends and allies I'd met along the way. To the strangers who'd taken a chance on me, who had affirmed what I'd guessed about us humans. I spoke their names to the wind. I waved at them, though I knew they could not see. And with my last bit of energy, shouted to the millions below that I had made it, sounding my celebratory yap over the rooftops of the world. That there was nothing I could not do, nothing *we* could not do if we learned to trust each other, nothing we could not change if we learned to ask each other for the strength we did not have alone, nothing that we need fear if we have each other. The wind caught my shirt, cooled my face, and with my arms above me, the hill beneath me, I felt in that moment what I'd never felt before: if I wanted to, I could fly.

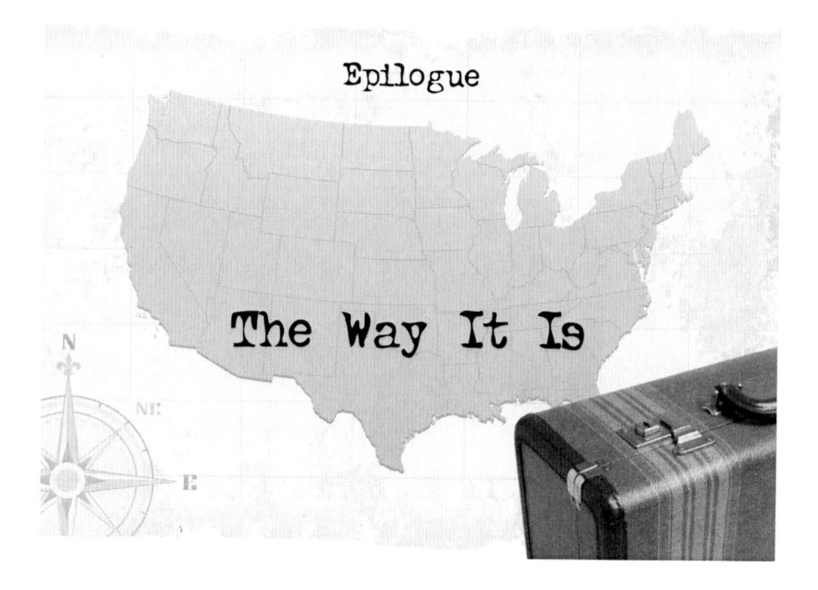

Epilogue

The Way It Is

Whatever you can do, or dream you can, begin it.
Boldness has genius, power, and magic in it.

—*Goethe*

Whenever I tell my story, or even part of it, people want to know: what did I learn? It's certainly hard to sum up concisely. There's so much to say. What didn't I learn? Everything changed over that trip, and even this book could only contain a fraction of the conversations I had, and the ideas I discovered—or that discovered me.

So I usually settle for one answer when asked what I learned: we all possess the seeds of greatness.

We've defined greatness as wealth, fame, power, influence. But true greatness is simply goodness. There is nothing more powerful, nothing more truly great, than helping a human being in a time of need. In our small acts we become great to one another. Each of us has the intrinsic potential to be immense.

There are a few great men, like Nelson Mandela, Winston Churchill, Robert F. Kennedy, Martin Luther King, Jr., Gandhi, and others, who show us that breaking free of our own limitations is not only possible but essential to living a full and courageous life. For many years I have been one of the people who felt that his life was meaningless and his ability to rise up beyond his own mediocrity, impossible. I spent my life telling myself that living a full life was only meant for a select few. I was convinced I was not one of the "lucky ones" and I was fated to sit on the sidelines feeding off the scraps of the chosen few. This trip taught me one thing: fuck that!

It showed me that if we stay stuck in our old mediocre lives we are doomed. It showed me that being bold can create great change in your life and that of others. It showed me that if I stayed small I was going to suffer. It showed me that we are all one. It showed me that sometimes we have to be willing to take risks to achieve great things. It showed me that we can't do this alone. It showed me that we are all able to make changes to our lives.

At this moment, guns are being fired in hate and in defense, somewhere a man is making a bomb, and somewhere the world is cracking in a new place. But here, and now, the cracks in the world can start to be mended; the fissure can begin to be fixed. We can sew one another up, and heal the wounds we've caused and felt, if only we'd each of us see every human connection as an amazing adventure worth the risk. Finding human connections in small ways is the only way to solve the bigger problems.

I used to feel each man was an island. How wrong I was. We are not. In fact we are tethered to each other with invisible bonds that no man or circumstance can break. Our ability to function successfully in the world depends on our ability to connect with each other. We are one.

Upon my arrival in Los Angeles, I recovered for a few days, called my family, and went to a doctor, who was somewhat displeased with my experiment (though I think in the end, he too was won over.) Within a week, I had a business plan in place for a production company, and within three months, I'd sold *Amazing Adventures* to National Geographic, eventually resulting in three seasons, broadcast in over 100 countries around the world. Amazing adventures indeed.

And yes, I saw Katherine again. But that's another story. As much hers to tell as mine.

I speak to my father once a week, and though he's slapped me on the back and told me he's proud, I'm pretty sure he still doesn't fully understand what I do or why. We're different people, and that's okay. What I now know is who I am, and that makes all the difference.

I still keep in touch with a few of the kind strangers I met along the way. I was able to track down a few of them and say thanks, and we exchange Christmas cards and e-mails. But some of the most important are ghosts to me, or angels. They appeared at just the right moment, and then continued on the road, where they'll help someone else, I am sure.

Last year, I actually made it down to Argentina, and took a couple of weeks to travel in the footsteps of Che Guevera. I didn't do it on a motorcycle, or with a companion. But I looked over the green mountains and across the blue rivers, and into the eyes of the people I met in small villages and large cities. And in each place, I saw what I'd seen in the plains and hills and the people of the United States, Europe, and beyond: promise, beauty, and hope.

And today, I do what I said I would do. I run a television production company that focuses on creating adventure travel shows, inspiring others to do what I did, to step outside their cells and comfort zones. I am a freelance journalist who writes adventure travel articles, and I'm a host who appears on TV shows about travel and inspiration. I'm trying, in a small way, to be Che to someone else. This book is my motorcycle diary, waiting for someone to discover . . .

About the Author

Leon Logothetis is an experienced television host and producer. Over the past few years, he has starred in a number of TV series, including three seasons of *Amazing Adventures of a Nobody,* which aired internationally on the National Geographic Channel. He has also been featured on the popular MTV series *MADE* and on Discovery Europe's travel show *Destination Future.* Leon also runs his own production company, Shankly Productions. As a TV producer, he has created large-scale TV series for channels such as National Geographic and The Travel Channel, among others. Leon has been featured on dozens of news outlets, including CNN, Fox News, BBC, and many more. He writes regularly for the *Los Angeles Times, Outside Magazine, Psychology Today,* and pens a blog on the *Huffington Post.*

Leon currently resides in Los Angeles, C.A., with his beloved Boston terrier, Winston Churchill.

For more information, or to contact Leon, please visit: www.leonlogothetis.com.

Book Club Discussion Questions

- Watching *The Motorcycle Diaries* inspired Leon to make radical change in his life. What movie, book, or other factors have been sources of radical transformation for you? Discuss in what ways they changed your life.

- To prepare for his journey, Leon divests himself of the things we believe to be necessities for everyday life (car, money, cell phone, etc.). If you had to choose two things to divest yourself of—if even for just a month or two—what would they be? Why?

- Gene (the older gentleman Leon meets on the train to Charleston) prefers to travel by train because it gives him time to meet people along the way. Is this something you would consider doing—changing the way you travel in order to experience "travel" on a different level? Explore your thoughts and feelings about this.

- How do you feel or react when a stranger approaches you when traveling? Have the stories in this book changed your views about this? Explore your thoughts about this.

- How far would you go in helping a stranger? Would you go so far as Julie, who gave Leon her house keys? What would make you lay down your barriers for a total stranger?

- In many ways, the book is about reinventing yourself. In what ways does travel truly allow us the ability to do this?

- What does it mean to trust our fellow humans? Explore the levels of trust and the barriers we set up in our interactions with others.

- Thinking about the homeless family Leon met in Indianapolis, do you agree with Leon that happiness can be found in the most dire of circumstances, in this case homelessness? Why or why not?

- How, if at all, has Leon's account of his travels changed the way you view traveling? Will it change the way you take your next vacation, for example?

- At every turn of his journey, Leon encountered generous people, ready to help him in one form or another. Was this surprising to you? Why?

Other Books by Bettie Youngs Book Publishers

The Maybelline Story . . . and the Spirited Family Dynasty Behind It

Sharrie Williams

A woman's most powerful possession is a man's imagination.
—Maybelline ad, 1934

In 1915, when a kitchen-stove fire singed his sister Mabel's lashes and brows, Tom Lyle Williams watched in fascination as she performed what she called "a secret of the harem"—mixing petroleum jelly with coal dust and ash from a burnt cork and applying it to her lashes and brows. Mabel's simple beauty trick ignited Tom Lyle's imagination, and he started what would become a billion-dollar business, one that remains a viable American icon after nearly a century. He named it Maybelline in her honor.

Throughout the twentieth century, the Maybelline company inflated, collapsed, endured, and thrived in tandem with the nation's upheavals. Williams—to avoid unwanted scrutiny of his private life—cloistered himself behind the gates of his Rudolph Valentino Villa and ran his empire from a distance. Now, after nearly a century of silence, this true story celebrates the life of an American entrepreneur, a man whose vision rocketed him to success along with the woman held in his orbit Evelyn Boecher—who became his lifelong fascination and muse. Captivated by her "roaring charisma," he affectionately called her the "real Miss Maybelline" and based many of his advertising campaigns on the woman she represented: commandingly beautiful, hard-boiled, and daring. Evelyn masterminded a life of vanity, but would fall prey to fortune hunters and a mysterious murder that even today remains unsolved.

A fascinating and inspiring story, a tale both epic and intimate, alive with the clash, the hustle, the music, and dance of American enterprise.

A richly told juicy story of a forty-year, white-hot love triangle that fans the flames of a major worldwide conglomerate.
—Neil Shulman, associate producer, *Doc Hollywood*

ISBN: 978-0-9843081-1-8 • $18.95

Out of the Transylvania Night

Aura Imbarus

An epic tale of identity, love, and the indomitable human spirit.

Communist dictator Nicolae Ceausescu had turned Romania into a land of zombies as surely as if Count Dracula had sucked its lifeblood. Yet Aura Imbarus dares to be herself: a rebel among the gray-clad, fearful masses. Christmas shopping in 1989, Aura draws sniper fire as Romania descends into the violence of a revolution that topples one of the most draconian regimes in the Soviet bloc. With a bit of Hungarian mysticism in her blood, astonishingly accurate visions lead Aura into danger—as well as to the love of her life. They marry and flee a homeland still in chaos. With only two pieces of luggage and a powerful dream, they settle in Los Angeles where freedom and sudden wealth challenge their love as powerfully as Communist tyranny.

Aura loses her psychic vision, heirloom jewels are stolen, a fortune is lost, followed by divorce. But their early years as lovers in a war-torn country and their rich family heritage is the glue that reunites them. They pay a high price for their materialistic dreams, but gain insight and a love that is far richer. *Out of the Transylvania Night* is a deftly woven narrative about finding greater meaning and fulfillment in both free and closed societies.

> Aura's courage shows the degree to which we are all willing to live lives centered on freedom, hope, and an authentic sense of self. Truly a love story!
>
> **—Nadia Comaneci, Olympic gold medalist**

> If you grew up hearing names like Tito, Mao, and Ceausescu but really didn't understand their significance, read this book!
>
> **—Mark Skidmore, Paramount Pictures**

> This book is sure to find its place in memorial literature of the world.
>
> **—Beatrice Ungar, editor-in-chief, Hermannstädter Zeitung**

ISBN: 978-0-9843081-2-5 • $14.95

In bookstores everywhere, online, or from the publisher:
www.BettieYoungsBooks.com

On Toby's Terms

Charmaine Hammond

When Charmaine and her husband adopted Toby, a five-year-old Chesapeake Bay retriever, they figured he might need some adjusting time, but they certainly didn't count on what he'd do in the meantime. Soon after he entered their lives and home, Toby proved to be a holy terror who routinely opened and emptied the hall closet, turned on water taps, pulled and ate things from the bookshelves, sat for hours on end in the sink, and spent his days rampaging through the house. Oddest of all was his penchant for locking himself in the bathroom, and then pushing the lid of the toilet off the tank, smashing it to pieces. After a particularly disastrous encounter with the knife-block in the kitchen—and when the couple discovered Toby's bloody paw prints on the phone—they decided Toby needed professional help. Little did they know what they would discover about this dog.

On Toby's Terms is an endearing story of a beguiling creature who teaches his owners that, despite their trying to teach him how to be the dog they want, he is the one to lay out the terms of being the dog he needs to be. This insight would change their lives forever.

> Simply a beautiful book about life, love, and purpose.
> **—Jack Canfield, Coauthor *Chicken Soup for the Soul* series**

> In a perfect world, every dog would have a home and every home would have a dog—like Toby!
> **—Nina Siemaszko, actress, *The West Wing***

> This is a captivating, heartwarming story and we are very excited about bringing it to film.
> **—Steve Hudis, Producer, IMPACT Motion Pictures**

ISBN: 978-0-9843081-4-9 • $14.95

In bookstores everywhere, online, or from the publisher:
www.BettieYoungsBooks.com

Diary of a Beverly Hills Matchmaker

Marla Martenson

The inside scoop from the Cupid of Beverly Hills, who has brought together countless couples who have gone on to live happily ever after. But for every success story there are ridiculously funny dating disasters with high-maintenance, out-of-touch, impossible to please, dim-witted clients!

Marla takes her readers for a hilarious romp through her days as an L.A. matchmaker and her daily struggles to keep her self-esteem from imploding in a town where looks are everything and money talks. From juggling the demands her out-of-touch clients, to trying her best to meet the capricious demands of an insensitive boss, to the ups and downs of her own marriage to a Latin husband who doesn't think that she is "domestic" enough, Marla writes with charm and self-effacement about the universal struggles all women face in their lives. Readers will laugh, cringe, and cry as they journey with her through outrageous stories about the indignities of dating in Los Angeles, dealing with overblown egos, vicariously hobnobbing with celebrities, and navigating the wannabe-land of Beverly Hills. In a city where perfection is almost a prerequisite, even Marla can't help but run for the Botox every once in a while.

Marla's quick wit will have you rolling on the floor.
—Megan Castran, international YouTube Queen

Sharper than a Louboutin stiletto, Martenson's book delivers!
—Nadine Haobsh, *Beauty Confidential*

Martenson's irresistible wit is not to be missed.
—Kyra David, author, *Lust, Loathing, and a Little Lip Gloss*

ISBN: 978-0-9843081-0-1 • $14.95

In bookstores everywhere, online, or from the publisher:
www.BettieYoungsBooks.com

Living with Multiple Personalities

Christine Ducommun

Christine Ducommun eloquently shares her story of her descent into madness, struggling to regain her sanity as four personalities vie for control of her mind and protect her from the demons of her childhood. A story of identity, courage, healing, and hope.

Christine Ducommun was a happily married wife and mother of two, when—after returning to live in the house of her childhood—she began to experience night terrors, a series of bizarre flashbacks, and "noises in her head."

Eventually diagnosed with dissociative identity disorder (DID), Christine's story details an extraordinary twelve-year ordeal of coming to grips with the reemergence of competing personalities her mind had created to help her cling to life during her early years.

Therapy helps to reveal the personalities, but Christine has much work to do to grasp their individual strengths and weaknesses and understand how each helped her cope and survive her childhood as well as the latent influences they've had in her adult life. Fully reawakened and present, the personalities struggle for control of Christine's mind and her life tailspins into unimaginable chaos, leaving her to believe she may very well be losing the battle for her sanity. Christine's only hope to regain her sanity was to integrate each one's emotional maturity while jettisoning the rest, until at last their chatter in her head could cease.

Anyone who has ever questioned themselves—whether for a day, a week, or longer—will find themselves in this stunning probe into the often secret landscape of the mind.

A powerful and shocking true story. Spellbinding!

—Josh Miller, Producer,
The Christine Ducommun Story,
(a made for TV movie)

ISBN: 978-0-9843081-5-6 • $14.95

In bookstores everywhere, online, or from the publisher:
www.BettieYoungsBooks.com

It Started with Dracula
The Count, My Mother, and Me

Jane Congdon

The terrifying legend of Count Dracula, silently skulking through the Transylvania night may have terrified generations of filmgoers, but the tall, elegant vampire captivated and electrified a young Jane Congdon, igniting a dream to one day see his mysterious land of ancient castles and misty hollows.

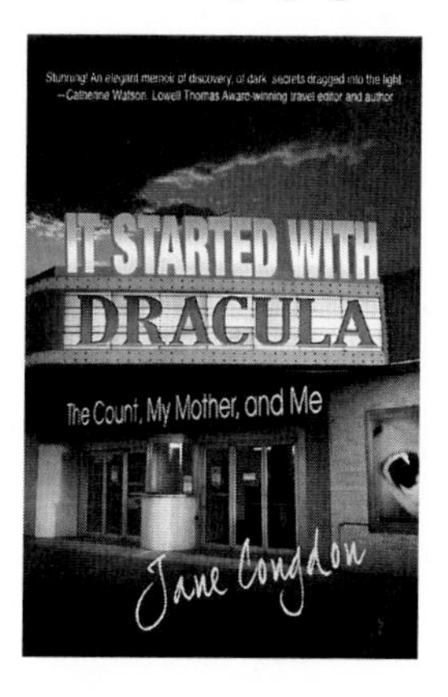

Four decades later, she finally takes her long-awaited trip—never dreaming that it would unearth decades-buried memories of life with an alcoholic mother. Set in Dracula's backyard, the story unfolds in a mere eighteen days as the author follows the footsteps of Dracula from Bucharest to the Carpathian Mountains and the Black Sea. Dracula's legend becomes the prism through which she revisits her childhood, and lays claim to a happiness she had never known.

A memoir full of surprises, Jane's story is one of hope, love—and second chances.

Unfinished business can surface when we least expect it. It Started with Dracula is the inspiring story of two parallel journeys: one a carefully planned vacation and the other an astonishing and unexpected detour in healing a wounded heart.

—Charles Whitfield, MD, bestselling author of *Healing the Child Within*

An elegant memoir of discovery, of dark secrets dragged into the light.

—Catherine Watson, Lowell Thomas Award-winning travel editor and author

An elegantly written and cleverly told real-life adventure story, proving that the struggle for self-love is universal. An electrifying read.

—Diane Bruno, CISION Media

ISBN: 978-1-936332-10-6 • $15.95

In bookstores everywhere, online, or from the publisher:
www.BettieYoungsBooks.com

Bettie Youngs Books

We specialize in MEMOIRS
. . . books that celebrate
fascinating people and
remarkable journeys